FEB -- '06

APPOINTMENT WITH DANGER

APPOINTMENT WITH DANGER:

Medical Care Can Kill You

Louise Lane

Copyright © 2004 by Louise Lane.

Library of Congress Number:		2004094151
ISBN :	Hardcover	1-4134-5942-0
	Softcover	1-4134-5941-2

This book was printed in the United States of America.

To order additional copies of this book, contact:
Xlibris Corporation
1-888-795-4274
www.Xlibris.com
Orders@Xlibris.com
25416

CONTENTS

Chapter

1 Introduction 11
2 Selecting A Doctor..19
3 Doctor/Patient Relationship 23
4 Diagnostic Procedures & Tests......................................27
5 Hospital Entry...37
6 Surgery...55
7 Selected Hospital Problems 61
8 Practice On The Dying..67
9 Medical Experimentation 69
10 Euthanasia 71
11 Life Or Death Blackboard 75
12 Legalized Suicide 77
13 Malpractice, Mishaps & Murder
   (48 Cases) 79
14 Patients' Bill of Rights & A Health Care
   Proxy Form..115
15 Conclusion-Prescription for a Healthy Life 121

Index 135
Drugs 139

This book is dedicated to my father.

1

Introduction

"Do the sick no harm."
Florence Nightingale

Did you ever think that one routine, casual office visit to a doctor can destroy your health, your eyesight, and maybe even your life? Well it can, and it has at the hands of doctors in their offices, as well as in medical centers and hospitals they work in all across America.

Every day, doctors kill their patients by administering risky or unnecessary but monetarily rewarding tests, unsafe drugs and procedures, medical errors, incorrect diagnosis, inept and careless, sub-standard treatment. Over 98,000 died last year because of medical malpractice. Iatrogenically caused (doctor-caused) injuries, illness or diseases result in more deaths than are caused by crime, wars, AIDS, smoking, illegal drugs, and automobile accidents. In hospitals alone, the thousands of malpractice-related deaths are not often accidentally caused. Negligence, inadequate knowledge, callousness, and bungling errors rule the medical scene.

A "Universal Protocal" featuring new rules for all of our nation's hospitals as of July 1, 2004, has been designed to prevent "wrong-site surgery," operating on the wrong person, and performing the wrong procedure on anyone. It includes strict guidelines for marking surgical incisions, verifying the type and locations of the surgery, and the identity of the patient. The whole surgical team must verify all relevant documents and review them before an operation. The site of the incision must be marked clearly in an "unambiguous" manner with an indelible marker. It may have the doctors' initials or the word, "yes." Then immediately preceding the surgery, the entire surgical team must take a "time-out" before starting, to check with each member and the patient, to make sure that it is the right person getting the operation, the exact site of surgery, and that it is the correct operation. The Joint Commission on Accreditation of Healthcare Organizations "will apply a zero-tolerance policy to noncompliance," said the commission's spokesperson Mark Forstneger. The penalty for violation of the new rules is loss of accreditation.

The new Protocol comes too late for many patients. The field of medicine is more of an applied art, than a science. Therefore, it is up to you, the patient, to decide if a treatment is safe, knowing that medical care can still kill you.

Why is it difficult for the medical consumer to avoid incompetent, inept, careless, callous, bungling, impaired, uncaring and inexperienced doctors? One reason is that justice moves slowly. Cases take years to go through disciplinary procedures or the court system, and taking the dangerous doctor to court is no guarantee of a successful case against him. To make matters worse, most doctors are reluctant to testify against their colleagues, and many juries falsely think of doctors as gods who can do no wrong and are not deliberately malevolent. Lastly, dead patients tell no tales: They cannot speak out. While a doctor is under investigation, his name is usually kept confidential and the public does not, therefore, have any knowledge about this potentially dangerous doctor until charges are finally levied against him or her. During all that time—it could take a few years—the doctor usually continues in his medical practice. Even when dangerous doctors are disciplined for negligence and convicted, some of them will just move to another state and continue to put more patients at risk of great harm. Your case may not even be taken by a law firm—because they are generally only looking for the big dollar amounts of wrongful death cases. Fewer law firms will take your case if you're still alive or somewhat recovered from a doctor's negligence or deliberate malpractice. In addition, the doctors might say you caused your own injuries, or that your problems are due to the illness and not to anything they did to you. Yes—doctors cover-up their mistakes, they bury their mistakes, they deny their errors, and they hide behind their pure white uniforms. To see how some of them operate, watch the movie, "The Verdict." The doctors are not so pure, and many have long ago forgotten the original Hippocratic Oath, which advises them not to do any harm.

Remember the saying "Caveat Emptor"—let the buyer beware? The same thing applies to a visit to the doctor's office when you are a buyer of medical services. As a consumer (patient), you cannot be careful enough, because when you go to a doctor's medical office, there is the clear potential for danger ahead. The more visits, the more harm may be done to you by repeated, possibly harmful tests. The Rand Corporation several years ago reported that as much as "one-fourth to one-third of medical care is unwarranted or of debatable value."

Consult your own health and financial or other advisors after reading this book, but "Heal Thyself" is something to be looked into. Educate yourself by reading books, accessing the Internet and research journals, which offer the latest information on the condition you've been told you have.

Always remember that under the United States Constitution, a patient has an absolute right to refuse medical treatment. This right has been reinforced in court rulings. It has also been ruled that even if a patient's refusal of treatment may lead to death, a person still has the right to refuse any medical treatment that he or she does not want.

There are criminal personalities who hide out in the physicians' white uniforms of purity. But they are not so pure. They are secretly devious and sinister, and operate under the 'safety' of their white coats and prestigious title of 'Doctor.' Yet they have their wicked ways, callousness, carelessness with medical procedures, use of harmful, hazardous diagnostic tests, and overall rough physical examinations, which are not without their consequences. And instead of criminal prosecution for clearly criminal acts, which they may perpetrate on a patient, in most cases the patient is left in the precarious position of suing for medical malpractice. I say precarious, because if you do not lose an arm, a leg, brain function, or your life—because of a doctor's malpractice, your case may not be taken.

The word of warning in the title of this book is meant to alarm, yes, alarm—and caution all Americans to beware of any and all physical examinations and 'treatments' employed by doctors in their offices or hospitals, whether these 'treatments' or 'tests' are invasive or not. If they are invasive one is advised to think hard and long about it before submitting. To agree in haste can be disastrous. Remember this: a doctor must tell you in advance what he is going to do and have your informed consent before doing any medical or invasive procedure. You, therefore, accept responsibility for the refusal. The doctor may not force his will against yours. To avoid any problems, you should say, "What procedures are you planning to do, because I want you to tell me in advance." "Are there any complications or hazards from your tests?" Ask what the tests will show him, and if his machine is accurate. Ask if there are any side effects or risks possible as a result of these tests. "What costs are involved with each of the tests?" In hospitals as well as doctors' offices, many needless, expensive and harmful procedures are done. To protect yourself, never go to a doctor's office alone.

Many times excessive numbers of blood tests are done in doctors' offices as well as in hospitals. In a hospital, the average patient has blood taken more than once a day. Unnecessary and potentially dangerous blood transfusions are done on patients who have barely given any consent for them. The potential for the transfer of the HIV virus is there, as well as possibly deadly bacteria. Patients should be assertive in declining routine transfusions or excessive blood tests. Repeated blood tests weaken a person, and tend to lower a person's immune system; and when blood tests are given after a person has fasted over-night or has been dehydrated for many hours, the risk of a stroke rises significantly. One of the reasons that doctors give tests which are not necessary and may be harmful, is the practice of 'defensive medicine.' They may fear lawsuits, so they overdo medical protocols, and the risks affect the life and health of the individual patient.

This book will focus on "Just the facts" and will

discuss which tests or procedures to beware of, to avoid, or to think about and ponder in advance of your decision. Remember, it's your body and your life that is at stake.

If the doctor harms you, in most cases little will happen to him (except in death cases, brain trauma, loss of limbs). He will virtually get slapped on the wrist and perhaps change his location. All the lifetime of suffering and dire consequences of his actions (which in many cases will be difficult for you to actually prove in court) will remain with you for a long time—or for the rest of your life. Another section of this book will present cases where 'routine' medical procedures, tests or physical examinations harmed people and caused them to suffer for the rest of their lives, or caused their deaths. The moral is: PATIENTS BEWARE!

Why are physical examinations so full of danger? This book will discuss the reasons for this and at least some of the known consequences of different types of examinations and 'routine' procedures and tests. Also in this book (Chapter 13), you will read about factual cases of people who suffered pain, damage to their bodies and health, and death. Some cases will include the names of people involved, while others are listed anonymously. However, all cases are real.

2

Selecting A Doctor

What qualities should you look for in selecting a doctor? The attributes of a good doctor for you should certainly include someone who is a caring, sympathetic, understanding and concerned individual. He or she should be someone who is open, willing to listen, share information, and communicate with you. If the doctor has an assembly-line office setup and is unwilling to give you the attention, respect, and time you need, then that doctor may be one to avoid.

Being board-certified is a minimum requirement you should look for. It was recently estimated that there are about 10,000 phony doctors operating in the United States with fraudulent credentials. They've done many types of operations and procedures to unsuspecting patients, often with deadly results.

A young doctor might be more aware of the latest information and updated medical techniques than an older doctor, but he might also make you the subject of a greater number of unnecessary tests and procedures by which to increase your bill and payments to him. This helps him to repay the costs of his new medical practice. So you, the patient, can sometimes suffer a lifetime of painful consequences as a result of this doctor's unnecessary and risky or harmful tests. Young doctors are not only paying back the debts from their school training, they are often buying an expensive home and starting a family. Patients beware! Medical consumers beware!

Once you have set up your list of doctors, ask friends if they have heard of any of these doctors or if they have other doctors to recommend in your area or elsewhere. Important questions to ask are: "Is the doctor communicative?" "Can you talk to him?" "Does he talk?" "Is he reliable?" "What are his fees?" "Do you have to wait a long time in his waiting room?" "How long?" "Do you have to sit and wait for forty minutes or more in his examination rooms, with one assistant after another, before the doctor will see you?" This is not a good sign. "Does he listen to the patient's conversation without any comments whatsoever?" If you feel the doctor is not listening to you, be persistent and make your concerns known. Studies have shown that you will receive better care from forthright questions to the doctor. A clear, open-ended physician/patient 'interview' is of utmost importance to the medical outcome.

Before going to a doctor's appointment, write down all the things you are going to tell him with regard to your symptoms so that you can cover all bases and yet be brief and to the point at once. You should also let him know about your past illnesses, allergies, operations and results. Often, this is written on the 'Registration Sheets' given to patients as they enter a doctor's office for the first time. There are usually questions about your family medical history, your own health and dietary habits, your occupation, a listing of any medications or drugs you are taking, and any allergies you have to foods or medicines. These preliminary registration sheets then become part of your records at the doctor's office. If he is a reliable practitioner he will have looked at these sheets before seeing you in his office.

If a drug is prescribed for you, ask why you need the drug and what it will do. Ask if a natural remedy is available instead of the drug. Ask if the drug has been on the market a long time. Ask if a generic drug (instead of the brand name) is available which would be cheaper. Ask if there are any known side effects. Ask how long the healing process can be expected to take. Ask about the time of day or evening to take the medicine, and whether to take it before, after, or with a meal. Also ask if there are any food interactions to be aware of with the medication, or any contraindications due to other drugs you may be taking for other conditions you may have. It is important to repeat this even if you've already noted your other illnesses or drugs on the 'Registration Sheet' when you entered the doctor's office. Always read the doctor/patient sheet that comes with a drug. If the pharmacist gives you a drug without it, tell him you want it. Most times they can access it on their computers and give you the printout.

Trouble begins when doctors have a rush-rush assembly-line practice with virtually seconds with each patient (after his assistants have done any preliminary tests). The 'trouble' can involve lifetime consequences.

3

Doctor/Patient Relationship

One main problem affecting the doctor-patient relationship is the doctor's inhumane attitude and inflated ego. Patients are often treated like uneducated or ignorant children. Often, a patient's wishes are deliberately ignored or superseded by the doctor's own ideas for no other reason than the doctor's own ego. His ego is more important to him than letting a patient know that he, the doctor, is wrong.

Many doctors are lacking in humanistic skills and often shame or humiliate patients. Physicians also feel that their time is more important than patients' time, and keep them waiting for hours beyond their appointment. A legal precedent has already been set in Florida where a man sued his doctor because he waited an excessive amount of time. He won his case.

When you are not comfortable with your doctor-patient relationship, it might be wise to find another doctor, first requesting copies of your records, which you can bring to the new doctor.

Many doctors withhold information and do not communicate fully with their patients. They do not give information unless asked, and then only in a limited fashion, often with less than totally honest answers. Part of the reason for this is the element of time. They live by the saying, "Time is money." Doctors make more money by shortening the amount of time and care they give a patient. With less time, the quality of care and communication may suffer.

When medical information is withheld from patients—as to their risks from procedures, knowledge about their illness, alternative procedures, or prognosis for recovery—the patient has lost control over his own destiny, his own mental and physical health.

Withheld information about adverse effects of certain tests, procedures or drugs used in the pregnancy and delivery process, for example, can lead to serious consequences for a new mother and her baby. In addition, research on withholding health information from patients has consistently been shown to have negative results such as anger, anxiety, depression, psychological withdrawal, 'cognitive neglect,' 'cognitive immobilization,' decreased compliance, apathy, passivity, acquired helplessness, increased reported pain, greater number of reported symptoms, higher morbidity, hypertension, heightened catecholamine excretion, adrenaline loss and elevated levels of hydrocortisone.

With the recommendation of a surgical procedure in a hospital, the doctor can make even more money, communicate less with the patient, and exert greater control over him. With each visit to the hospital, his fees add up; with each test he orders, he and the hospital can make more money by adding to the patient's bill. Who suffers like a guinea pig?

The patient is akin to a prisoner, unless he becomes an assertive individual. A patient has the right to complete and current information about his diagnosis, treatment and prognosis. He has the right to refuse any treatment, the right to privacy, and the right to refuse any experimental or risky procedure.

4

Diagnostic Procedures & Tests

Some diagnostic procedures, which have inherent dangers, are the following:

Some diagnostic procedures, which have inherent dangers, are the following:

1	Orthopedics	Bones misaligned. Excessive number of x-rays taken can lead to radiation overdose.
2	Angiography	Nicking other body organs.
3	Carotid Endarterectomy	Strokes from clots, death.
4	Transurethral Biopsies	Hemorrhage, tears.
5	Cervical Biopsies	Hemorrhage, tears, cancer.
6	Surgery of the Face	Numbness, bruising, death.
7	Liposuction	Hemorrhage, clots, embolism, death
8	Abdominal Surgery	Hemorrhage, infections; can lead to cancer later on.
9	Pregnancy and Childbirth	Excessive sonograms, amniocentesis may affect the fetus. Drugs and instruments may be harmful to the fetus and the mother.
10	Feeling for lumps, tumors in a 'general' physical exam—e.g. abdomen, etc.	Excessive pressure or 'digging' by the physician can result in lump formation, cancer.
11	Eye pressure tests for glaucoma, Eye gonioscopy tests, and invasive procedures—e.g. Cataract Surgery. Dark or dimly lit room, with flashlight focused suddenly on the eyes.	Can actually 'trigger' glaucoma in the eyes of people with elevated or higher than average IOP (Intraocular Pressure) or narrow eye angles. Blurred vision. Decreased sight. Double vision. Blindness.

12	Certain tests for which drugs are given to detect Kidney problems	
13	Mammograms	Depending on the machine, too much radiation may occur. Bruising of breasts can lead to lumps.
14	Stress Test	Heart Attack

In many doctors' offices there can be three to five assistants doing a variety of tests on patients before they are seen by the doctor. For example, in some Ophthalmologists' offices, three different technicians may test one patient's eye pressure. When the eye doctor ultimately comes in to see the patient, he also will do an intraocular (IOP) test on the patient. Thus, in a small amount of time, a person's eyes have been subjected to four pressure tests in succession, four doses of fluorescent dye and four doses of anesthetics for the eyes (usually Alcaine or Dexacaine), flashlights shining into the eyes, gonio lenses pressed against the naked eyes. This latter test (gonioscopy) can injure the eyes and cause some loss of peripheral vision. The gonio lens is pressed against the eyeball. Everyone should beware of submitting to this test, for which the doctor receives an extra fee. It is invasive and risky; you can lose some eyesight afterwards. An eye doctor should not do this (or the IOP) without the patient's consent, and a genuine need for it. Let no eye doctor tell you that his tests have no consequences. That is not true. A medical book warns, "Never put direct pressure on the eyeball."

Eye pressure tests themselves can raise a person's IOP, and that is true even if one does the test oneself using The Proview Eye Pressure Monitor by Bausch & Lomb. There is no valid reason why an eye doctor should do two tests at the same visit, unless he's unsure about his machine working. In that case, he should get another machine and stop risking the eyesight of patients. A person visiting an eye doctor should know that more than one pressure test is potentially extremely harmful. It has been known to actually trigger glaucoma, as can different chemicals, tests, operations and eye injuries. Sometimes just one test to determine a person's IOP can be dangerous and cause injury by disorienting the parts of the eye or creating an air pocket. It depends on the machine used, whether it's the puff of air type, the Goldmann Tonometer, the invasive Gonioscopy, the person administering the test, and the condition of the patient's eyes. In a person who has a family gene for glaucoma, a test might actually trigger it. This is especially true for people who have narrow angles in their eyes or narrow angle glaucoma. A sudden flash of a doctor's flashlight could trigger a glaucoma attack and loss of some sight within hours. The test always has consequences.

Some eye drops can also cause loss of peripheral vision, blurred central vision, and nearsightedness. An example of this is Pilocarpine, which also decreases night vision. Another eye drop, "Cosopt in a Solution of Mercury" contains mercury—a metal that takes years to leave the human body, and is a poison. Even if the drops are prescribed for one eye only, the drug affects the other eye as well as your entire body, because all drugs become systemic and go throughout the entire body.

Cortico-steroid drugs for eye inflammations and other disorders can trigger glaucoma in some people. Several glaucoma drugs are contraindicated if you have bradycardia, heart disease, cerebrovascular insufficiency, type II diabetes, hypotension, or kidney disease.

What constitutes healthy intraocular pressure is an individual thing. Someone with 16mm Hg may need surgery while others with 30mm Hg pressure may not need any treatment. In general, pressure between 8 to 22mm Hg is considered O.K. Any person's eye pressure or blood pressure can vary a lot during the day and night. According to the Glaucoma Research Foundation in San Francisco, "Recent studies show that just measuring eye pressure is not a reliable way to detect glaucoma. Eye pressure can go up and down during the day or in a month. Also some people's optic nerves are not damaged by high IOP, while others' optic nerves are damaged by relatively low pressure." At the very least, beware of visits to the eye doctor. "Never trouble trouble until trouble troubles you." Never have a dilated eye exam or flashlights in your eyes if you have narrow angles or narrow angle glaucoma. You will probably have a glaucoma attack in the affected eye within hours.

Glaucoma can also be triggered by other doctor-caused interventions such as cataract operations. Even though there are new and improved procedures for removing a cataract, the operation can still induce glaucoma—a lifelong condition. It can happen because any eye injury or surgery can cause a slight change or variation of the parts inside the eye. Any of the parts, such as the ciliary body, the iris, the pupil, scar tissue or trapped air can then block the passageway by which intraocular fluid flows. Invasive eye examinations, eye surgeries, stressful situations, and repeated eye pressure tests at one office visit, may raise your intraocular pressure, cause vision loss, and trigger glaucoma. Stress from over-testing of the eyes and some chemicals can also cause eyelid atrophy (ptosis)— not a pretty sight. However, glaucoma is far worse, as it is a lifetime ticket leading to blindness if it is unable to be controlled. Many patients become blind due to inept or unsuccessful treatments by eye doctors.

Lots of tests and hazardous medical procedures do not spell safety for the patient. A lens pressed hard against your eyeball will not do any good for your eyesight afterwards. Flashlights shining closely into your eyes will also not help your vision. Since most doctors do not give advance warning for these tests, or ask for your informed consent before invasive tests, you must speak up ahead of time to make your wishes known to the doctor and his staff.

Self-treatment for the eyes, besides a good daily vitamin with Lutein and Zeaxanthin is to eat spinach, kale, sweet potatoes, carrots, corn, peanuts, yellow peppers, red grapes, strawberries, oranges and kiwi fruit. The mineral Manganese is supposed to reduce eye pressure, but is not advised in doses over 20 mg. It might damage the liver. It is better to eat it in foods e.g. peanuts. Bilberry has been said to improve eyesight. It is a 'cousin' of the blueberry, which is more widely available. It is preferable to find your vitamins in foods, and to drink pure water.

Another excessive use of a potentially harmful diagnostic test is that of x-rays taken by doctors, technicians, and dentists. The x-rays increase your medical bills, rob the insurance companies, and put patients at risk from excessive radiation, which is cumulative in the body.

If more x-rays are taken than are actually needed, the excessive x-rays are potentially cancer causing and are the basis of about 90 percent of man-made doses of radiation given to people, according to the National Academy of Sciences. They have said that this amount should be decreased by half through better "technical and educational methods."

Doctors and hospitals try to recover their investment for the high cost of the x-ray machines by over-using them. Patients are then put at risk of developing cancer. According to the authors of "Ionizing Radiation: Health Hazards of Medical Uses,"** x-rays are "potentially the most harmful" of all nonsurgical diagnostic tests. Older machines expose patients to more radiation. Heavier or more muscular people need higher x-ray voltages, thus subjecting them to greater harm. They say that doctors often abuse the use of x-rays, whether of the chest, skull, abdomen, gallbladder, upper G.I. tract or a barium-assisted procedure. The latter three are the most abused.

You should always ask if an x-ray is absolutely necessary. MRI (magnetic resonance imaging) tests are preferable to CAT scans (CT scans) due to the latter's radiation, but you may not really need that. Radiation on the body is cumulative. Fluoroscopy is not recommended for any healthy person. Children should not be exposed to repeated or multiple-view x-rays. It is very dangerous for them to be exposed to radiation. Everyone should always have lead barrier shields covering areas of the body that are not involved with the particular area to be x-rayed. Radiation can be deadly to the thyroid, breasts, bone marrow and reproductive organs. The x-ray machines should be new, and have high-speed film.

In conclusion, x-ray radiation—as is all radiation, even from cell phones—is cumulative. Are you willing to risk the x-ray exposure on yourself? Will the 'benefit' really outweigh the risk? Where hospitals are more patient-health conscious, routine chest or back x-rays are not given. They are certainly not recommended in normal pre-natal care, for people under 50, or for women under 50 who have no family history or symptoms of breast cancer, or older women with no symptoms.

Results of a Canadian study regarding mammogram tests were announced in September, 2002. The research project concluded that

mammograms "do not save lives." Depending on
the radiation emitted by the mammogram machine,
whether it's an old machine, and the amount of
pressure placed upon a woman's breasts, a
mammogram is capable of detecting as well as
possibly promoting breast cancer in a woman.

Are doctors giving their patients breast cancer?
Bruising can precipitate breast cancer. Breasts can
be pressed too hard against the mammogram
machine. Radiation also can cause cancer, so think
about it first, especially if you have no related
problems and have done a gentle, correct self-
examination. The FDA has said that mammography
should not be routinely done if there are no
symptoms or problems. Talk to your doctor as to
whether you want to hazard a machine-examination
(mammogram) and discuss it.

Whole-mouth x-rays done routinely or often,
are also very dangerous, as are all mouth x-rays.
Patients should indicate to their dentists that they
are concerned about whole-mouth x-rays taken at
once and they will tolerate dental x-rays only in the
area where they have a problem and only if the x-
ray is found to be entirely necessary—after a regular
dental examination.

If you move, or change dentists or doctors, always
request copies of your x-rays and records so that
you will not have to undergo the unnecessary,
hazardous radiation exposure and expensive tests
again.

The FDA has blamed thousands of cancer deaths

per year upon unnecessary x-rays. They have said that many x-rays are taken by poorly trained technicians who can accidentally expose a patient to one hundred times the needed dose of radiation. They say that if your lower back or abdomen is going to be x-rayed, you should ask for a lead shield to protect the sex organs.

I know of a woman who was being wheeled towards the operating room for an operation, when suddenly the technician said to her "I forgot to do the _____ x-rays." These x-rays would have represented a duplication of x-rays she had already taken in her doctor's office. Being an assertive woman, she said to the technician, "It's too late now. Forget it. You're not going to do them."

SOME SAMPLE DOSES of RADIATION in 'millirems':

Type	Total Body Dose	Bone Marrow Dose	Gonad Dose
Dental bite	5	1	0
Dental, Whole mouth	10-30	1	0
Chest	5-10	1	1
Abdominal	1150	110	25-120
Spine	1100-2200	85-165	22-300
Kidney (IVP)	500-1500	75	60-130
Upper GI Series	400-1300	34	12-80
Barium enema	500-2500	630	175-500
Liver scan	1500	N/A	N/A

| CT scan | 2000-6000 | N/A | N/A |
| Thyroid scan | 80,000 | N/A | N/A |

The famous 1950's television star, Molly Goldberg, went in to a New York medical center for diagnostic tests. She never came out alive. In a similar fashion, the giant Eddie Carmel went to Montefiore Hospital for tests, and died. This same type of thing, possible death by testing, has occurred to many others, but is not so well publicized. There is a test in which a tube is placed down a person's throat. Before the test is administered, the serious risks are spelled out on a consent form the patient must sign—if it is to be given. Patients beware. Know what you read, and then decide if you wish to take the risks involved, seek other alternatives, consult others, or learn more about your condition and how to ameliorate it.

5

Hospital Entry

If you have the misfortune or just plain bad luck to have to go to a hospital for an operation or any reason, you must be aware of many things: a possible abundance of filth and germs, a lack of cleanliness, violations of infection-control standards, endless blood tests, or any tests with non-sterile needles.

Even though modern technology has the capacity to check on blood safety, blood transfusions still hold the potential for danger to a patient. Transfusions may still cause the transmission of harmful bacteria or infectious diseases, even possibly the Hepatitis virus, AIDS, or other blood-borne illnesses. Moreover, excessive blood tests, especially when taken in a short period of time, can depress the immune system. When taken after a dehydrating fast or before breakfast, they can lead to a stroke.

You may acquire infectious bacteria from doctors,

nurses, or other hospital personnel who have first touched other seriously ill patients before touching you without washing their bare or gloved hands. In the year 2000, according to a report in the Chicago Tribune, about 103,000 people died after they contracted infections at the hospitals they went to for medical assistance. They also indicated that over seventy-five percent of all hospitals were mentioned as having "serious cleanliness and sanitation violations."

A patient may write a DNR order in advance, or give permission for a DNR to his Health Care Proxy Holder and sign it. A DNR—Do Not Resuscitate Order—refers only to receiving CPR: Cardio Pulmonary Resuscitation. It can involve mouth-to-mouth breathing and external chest massage, but can also continue with electric shock, a tube into a person's airway, or an injection of a medicine into the heart. Sometimes open-chest heart massage can be done. These drastic measures should be discussed with a doctor and family members, but you, the patient (or your guardian or Health Care Proxy Holder following your wishes) are the only one who has a right to make the decision about DNR ("No CPR").

The patient should think hard before wanting a DNR order, because the doctors may give you less than decent care, and withhold regular treatment. This neglect could cause you to die. A study in the Journal of the American Geriatric Society suggested that the patient's signature on a DNR order was like giving doctors' permission to avoid lifesaving care for that patient or even totally ignoring the person.

In another study, noted in the New England Journal of Medicine, one out of five Intensive Care nurses admitted to having speeded up the deaths of terminally ill patients—even without informing doctors, the families or the patients. The study results were released by Dr. David Asch of the University of Pennsylvania.

In 1989, a nurse, Richard Angelo, was convicted of killing four patients at Good Samaritan Hospital in West Islip, New York. The convictions were for murder for two deaths, manslaughter in another, and criminally negligent homicide in the fourth case. In a fifth case, he was found guilty of assaulting a patient who survived his assault.

Recently a hospital nurse, Charles Cullen, made a confession to killing at least 40 patients in Pennsylvania and New Jersey hospitals. It is said that he may have killed even more patients in medical facilities that he worked at, in other states.

There are too many times when one patient's chart with his type of operation may be mixed up with that of another patient of the same name. A woman in Florida with the same last name as another patient, died as a result of not receiving her diabetes medication because of a chart mix-up with the other woman. In New York, a man's wife saved her husband from having the wrong operation after she noticed his chart listed open-heart surgery when he was in the hospital for a prostate operation.

Another element of medical danger is the often careless, sloppy, and/or illegible handwriting of doctors in the writing of prescriptions or for instructions regarding a patient's care. This is a prescription for disaster, and lives have been sacrificed because of the misreading of drug dosages written by careless or callous doctors, and followed by hospital personnel who may not be careful enough. Inside a Boston hospital, some years ago, a young woman undergoing treatment for cancer, was accidentally given a deadly overdose of a drug, due to careless misreading of the prescribed dosage. This mistake killed the woman rapidly (see Chapter 13).

Many times, it is nurses who spot prescription errors made by doctors. A nationwide survey has shown that patients have more faith, trust and respect for nurses than for doctors. However, some nurses have admitted to raising the dosage of narcotics given to elderly patients to reduce their pain, and be "put out of misery." This has sometimes caused patient deaths.

Adding to a lack of good communication in hospitals is the enormous number of foreign nationals serving an intern residency in the U.S., or as doctors with J-1 Waiver status.

Drugs

The willy-nilly use of drugs to see which one will work and which will not is another medical issue regarding doctors' prescriptions inside of hospitals or in their medical offices. It is amazing that many doctors, ophthalmologists for example, are totally and completely unaware of the many systemic and life-altering or life-threatening side effects that many of their prescribed eye medications can cause: shortness of breath, low or high blood pressure, eye-lid atrophy, heart attacks, liver damage, nearsightedness, strange mouth-taste, clouded lens, blurred vision and blindness. They act totally dumbfounded when told about side effects of medications they dispense to their patients. In some cases, medications they prescribe will be clearly contraindicated regarding the disorder they are disbursing it for! Clearly, they have not done their homework regarding drugs.

Millions of patients each year suffer from medical complications due to drug-caused diseases and disasters. People are over-medicated to enlarge hospital bills and keep the drug companies in business. The result is shortened lives and many premature deaths. More than 5,000,000 hospital patients each year suffer from one or more instances of medical complications and bad consequences due to dangerous drugs and risky medical therapy. There are unknown and unexpected side effects and drug interactions that doctors are ignorant of, especially with new drugs and or various combinations of drugs given to the same individual. For example, alcohol affects most medications, and taken together with sedatives it can be deadly. Milk is to be avoided when taking the antibiotic Tetracycline. Broccoli interferes with the capabilities of blood thinners. Smoking can tend to make the blood clot. Long-term use of high dose steroid inhalers can cause glaucoma. Many antibiotics are prescribed without valid reasons. When given too long or too often, they can suppress a person's own immune system. According to Dr. Hobart Reimann, 15 to 30 percent of all patients given antibiotics will suffer from side effects, while many others will die from them. Antibiotics can cause rapid heart rate, aplastic anemia, leukopenia, high blood pressure, headaches, chills, fever, vomiting, diarrhea, rashes, dizziness, joint pain, decreased hearing, nerve swelling, kidney irritation, blurred vision, numbness and tingling of arms and legs, blood disorders, asthma, allergic psychosis, shock, weakness, sweating, severe bleeding, nerve damage, difficulty swallowing, colitis, toxic effects upon spleen, kidneys, the liver, and death. Recent research findings indicate that breast cancer can occur after long-term usage (e.g. fourteen years) of antibiotics.

If one truly needs antibiotics, some recommendations to be considered would be antibiotics for an appropriate number of days, followed by allowing the person's own immune system to work for a cure with pure water, vitamins (especially C & E), minerals (especially zinc), citrus fruits such as oranges, lemons and strawberries, and vegetables such as spinach, kale, cauliflower, tomato sauce, parsley, dill, and sweet potatoes. Some advocate boosting the immune system with Echinacea, an Alternative Medicine approach as opposed to traditional medicine of drugs. Avoid Third World fruits, as their plants are sprayed with pesticides that are banned in U.S. agriculture. Stay with American grown produce, and wash well.

Side effects from high blood pressure drugs may include excessive weight gain, insomnia, abdominal pain, depression and anxiety, dizziness, leukopenia, nervousness, fainting, shivering, angina pain, heart stress, nose bleed, skin eruptions, fatigue, muscle pain and weakness, damage to the brain, liver, and kidneys. Persons with excessively high blood pressure may need some medication. However, one can lower blood pressure by losing weight, avoiding salt, and eating bananas, baked potatoes, and apples.

Women who have high blood pressure, a history of migraine headaches, strokes or epilepsy should not take contraceptive pills. These pills can cause blood clots, pulmonary embolism, baldness, thrombophlebitis, jaundice, itching, heart problems, eye and vision disorders, cancerous growths, liver damage, diabetes, sterility, and death.

Anti-cholesterol drugs can cause muscle pain, hair loss, sweating, weight loss, nervousness, insomnia, fatigue, swelling, dizziness, ringing in the ears, hoarseness, headache, nausea, vomiting, indigestion, itching, skin rashes, menstrual irregularity, aggravation of existing heart disorders, frequent urination, changes in bowel habits, tremors, and increased metabolic rate.

Aspirin is known as an excellent clot-buster and blood thinner, and it is. Taken as low-dose therapy on a daily basis (81 mg. is a low dose) it is said to be an excellent way to prevent heart attacks and strokes. Some people prefer to take it in a higher dose, but every other day. It has also been shown to prevent colon cancer, according to the most recent research.

High doses of aspirin can cause gastrointestinal hemorrhage and bleeding, but this can be modified by using coated aspirin. Some side effects of high aspirin dosages may be ulcers, thirst, ringing in the ears, blurred vision, delirium, kidney disease, fetal death, stupor, mental retardation, skin eruptions, acidosis, rapid breathing and heartbeat, and worse.

Among the most abused types of drugs are sedatives and tranquillizers. Physicians routinely sedate their hospital patients. Sometimes it is done before MRI—magnetic resonance imagining exams. Many times these physicians will do this without the knowledge or consent of their patients. In most states, this is against the law. On the part of the doctors, it is pure arrogance and negligence to avoid informing patients of the risks involved with such sedation or tranquillization drugs, and to neglect to obtain their permission (Informed Consent) in advance. Doctors will tend to understate the harmful side effects of the drugs they want to inject into their patients, or have their patients ingest by mouth.

Tranquillizers and sedatives are very harmful drugs—for elderly persons, in particular. They are capable, even in relatively small doses, of doing major damage to an elderly person's heart, lungs, circulation, and central nervous system. Not only do sedatives and tranquillizers act as respiratory suppressants, but they also slow the heart rate, can cause heart destabilization and malfunction, low blood pressure, degeneration of heart muscle and blood vessels, enlargement of spleen and liver, fatty deposits in the liver, lungs, heart, and kidneys, shaking palsy, trembling, cataracts, myopia, lethargy, blurred vision, drowsiness, fatigue, blood disorders, dizziness, nausea, constipation, skin rashes, depression, convulsions, headache, dry mouth, heart palpitation, irritability, nasal stuffiness, dysarthria, ataxia, diarrhea, jaundice, mental disturbance, mental confusion, memory loss, personality changes, tremors, muscle twitching, allergic reactions, swelling in hands and feet, angioneurotic edema and vascular collapse, suicidal tendencies, habit forming, muscle paralysis, hypotonia, reduced reflexes, muscular weakness and lack of coordination.

The tranquillizing, weakening, and relaxing of the body's musculature, also includes relaxing and dilation of the laryngeal and esophageal muscles in the throat. A large dose of the sedation/tranquillization drugs may also destroy a person's ability to eat or to swallow food. Other consequences, which will most often occur with an overdose of these drugs, are loss of consciousness, coma, and death.

What is a moderate dose for one person may be a deadly dose for another—especially if the person is small, thin, and elderly. Drugs of this type, just like anesthesia, should take into account the person's size, weight, medical history, health considerations, age, and contraindications of the particular drug. Anyone, and hospital patients in particular, should beware of sleeping pills, sedatives, and tranquillizing drugs.

It is never wise to agree too quickly to allow yourself to be sedated or tranquillized. Tell your wishes to doctors and the hospital in advance, or write it on your Health Care Proxy form that you submitted to the hospital and doctors upon entry to the hospital. This is very important, because once you've been sedated, you cannot turn back the clock on its potential damages to your heart, your lungs, and weakened muscles. If you are a stroke patient, sedatives or tranquillizing drugs will immediately halt and delay the ability of your muscles to regain their previous strength and coordination. Your life itself will also be in jeopardy, especially if you are over 65 years of age, as the lowered respiration rate is not helpful for your life or health. It is also not helpful for anyone, at any age. In a hospital, you may acquire germs or bacteria, which will require your immune system to be very strong to fight the attack on your body. With lowered heart/respiration rates, in addition to the numerous blood tests given (possibly upsetting the electrolyte balance and decreasing the supply of red blood cells), patients are put at grave risk of death. Loss of blood through innumerable blood tests in hospitals tends to depress the immune system, and dangerously lower blood pressure. Patients are left highly susceptible to any and all kinds of germs that are in the hospital room or are carried into the room by traveling staff members. When not deemed to be entirely necessary, a blood test should be refused. It seems that doctors have not learned much since George Washington was almost bled to death—by doctors—and then died from this weakened condition, in 1799. In many emergency rooms/hospitals, seven to nine blood tests in succession may be given to one individual. An elderly person cannot make up the loss of this blood very easily or quickly. But this does not seem to deter doctors from their common practice of excessive blood tests. It also increases their bottom line, by way of bigger doctor/hospital bills.

Some examples of tranquillizers are **Valium, Librium, Xanax, and Tranxene**. Sleeping Pills are **Dalmane, Restoril, and Ambien**. Drugs such as these can cause addiction, memory loss, drug-induced unsteadiness (faltering gait), and mental impairment.

The drug Lorazepam, whose brand name is **Ativan**, belongs to a class of drugs called benzodiazepines. Lorazepam affects the chemicals in the brain in such a way that they may become unbalanced. Anxiety, nervous tension, dizziness and seizures may result. It should not be taken with alcohol, or very serious problems may occur. Pregnant or nursing women should avoid it, as should people with a history of depression, glaucoma, narrow-angle glaucoma, kidney, liver, asthma, bronchitis, emphysema or any respiratory problem. It is habit forming, and side effects are very likely to occur in any elderly person or anyone over 65 years of age. This includes unconsciousness, coma, and death. Ativan's side effects may increase when given with other drugs that cause drowsiness such as antidepressants, alcohol, antihistamines, sedatives, pain relievers, anxiety drugs, seizure drugs, sedatives and muscle relaxers. Many drugs are dangerous enough by themselves (e.g. Morphine is a respiratory suppressant), but when combined with others, the consequences can be deadly, and many side effects can occur which are not even expected. There are always drug interactions, allergic reactions, contraindications and adverse effects to consider before taking any drugs.

Many times drugs will adversely interact with foods, such as Tetracycline and milk. They can also interact with certain vitamins, minerals, herbal substances, or even foods such as grapefruits or grapefruit juice. Be careful with drugs, or as the old adage says, "Look before you leap."

One drug, which has been used to reduce brain damage from strokes, is Selfotel. In a study, patients improved in their ability to lead independent lives. Another drug, which is supposed to be given within 45 minutes or some say within a few hours following the onset of a stroke (CVA—cerebral vascular accident), is TPA—Tissue Plasminogen Activator (Streptokinase or Alteplase).

A new drug called Exanta, made by AstraZeneca, may be available now. With this drug in use, stroke patients should be able to avoid the Heparin and then Warfarin (Coumadin) drugs which are dangerous and require continuous 'monitoring' with endless blood tests on the patient.

Exanta does not require the continuous blood testing of the other drugs like Heparin, and it prevents blood clots as well or even better.

For self-care at home, stroke patients could use Exanta or aspirins. Check with your health care provider to decide, but remember, to avoid further strokes or brain damage, treatment should be immediate (preferably within minutes for a heart attack or stroke). With care at home, people are at *less* risk for pneumonia or other life-threatening illnesses easily acquired in a hospital, and are more comfortable in their own familiar surroundings. Then with home physical and other therapy, they can begin to walk again and to be independent. They should also avoid dehydration and use daily aspirin therapy as per the dosage recommended to them in accordance with their medical conditions.

The drug companies push drugs to doctors, and the doctors then push drugs to their patients. At big medical conventions, doctors are wined, dined and lectured to by speakers who advocate the benefits of the latest drugs from one company or another.

They've even touted drugs in advance of approval. The drug companies use subtle, clever marketing techniques to get doctors to prescribe their drugs, which is a major factor in the sky-high costs of drugs and health care.

What can you, a medical consumer, do to protect yourself regarding drug prescriptions for high blood pressure, arthritis, ulcers, high cholesterol, respiratory infections, etc.? You can ask the doctor to prescribe a generic version of the drug, instead of an expensive brand name, or perhaps an over-the-counter item. For example, if you have an upper respiratory infection, you can ask your doctor (if you've gone to one!) if non-drug, natural therapies could work just as well (e.g. drinking fluids, salt-water gargling, having hot chicken soup, taking aspirin, etc.).

For high blood pressure you might ask your doctor if a regimen of exercise, weight loss, calcium intake and a salt-restricted diet would work to bring your hypertension under control. Increasing potassium in your diet, by eating apples, almonds, bananas, oranges, potatoes, raisins and dried fruits could also help lower blood pressure.

There might be heart attack risks associated with some blood pressure medicines. A study has found that they should not be used routinely because of these hazards. The drugs involved, called calcium channel blockers, are: Nifedipine, Diltiazem and Verapamil, which are sold under a variety of brand names which include, Adalat, Calan, Cardizem, Dilacor, Isoptin, Procardia and Verelan.

Normally, beta-blockers and diuretics are used to lower high blood pressure. Researchers have found that these risks for heart attacks can occur in otherwise healthy people who are just taking these drugs to control hypertension. About fifty million Americans have high blood pressure, which puts them in increased danger of having a heart attack or a stroke. The drugs listed above are still being used, despite the new findings. In many cases, there are physicians who are unaware of the findings or have no new drugs to prescribe.

The study's author is Dr. Bruce Psaty, an epidemiologist at the University of Washington in Seattle, Washington and was funded by the National Institutes of Health.

How safe is the drug your doctor is prescribing? Several years ago, the chairman of the University of Minnesota's Medical School was producing, marketing and selling an anti-rejection drug, anti lymphocyte globulin (ALG) around the world. There were more than seventy-nine million dollars worth of sales from the drug. At least nine reactions to the drug were fatal, yet the federal Food and Drug Administration was never notified, as required. Patients were also not given any required information about that drug before giving their consent to use it. The chairman and a colleague were indicted regarding the above.

Drugs can save lives, but they can also destroy

them. Fifty-one percent of drug deaths are not amid addicts, but are among older people using prescription drugs. Even a slight overdose of Morphine given to a hospital patient can send him or her to the next world over-night.

Adverse drug reactions have reached huge proportions in the United States. There are lots of precautions regarding the side effects of each drug, and they are printed on the circulars inside the containers with the drug. If your pharmacist gives you a bottle without the drug company's circular, ask him for it.

It is very important to know the risks, the side effects and the contraindications of each drug you may take. Unfortunately, most doctors avoid telling patients what these side effects or possible complications may be. Often it's too late when a patient finds out what they are, e.g., the diet ingredient Ephedrine, which destroyed people's lives.

Since each person is a unique individual, a drug that may cause mild to serious side effects on one person may not have any perceivable adverse effects on another.

Elderly people may sometimes be taking several drugs concurrently, e.g., for arthritis, high blood pressure, depression, etc., and they must inform each doctor about their different medications. The doctors should be aware of contraindications of drugs, and which ones cannot be taken within a certain time frame with any other drug. If not, it is the medical consumer whose life is on the line.

The drug companies tend to exaggerate the benefits of their drugs and understate their side effects, according to the Medical Letter. The former medical director for Squibb Laboratories, Dr. Dale Console, said, "Doctors and the public are subjected to a constant 'barrage' of new drugs, some worthless and others with a greater potential for harm than good."

6

Surgery

When wondering whether or not to have surgery, think of the risks and benefits. In many cases, the benefits are unclear, but the risks are very real, possibly deadly. For example, while coronary bypass surgery is dangerous, a procedure called Carotid Endarterectomy, to clear out clogged carotid arteries, is even more risky. This operation can kill many more people than it saves. The New England Journal of Medicine warns against it. Fifteen percent of people who survived the operation had strokes afterwards, caused by this potentially fatal surgery.

In addition to costly tests, thousands of surgeons across the United States perform many needless operations. These operations are very expensive. They can also be painful and physically, emotionally, and mentally dangerous to the patient who agrees to have them. The only winner is the doctor who can then enlarge his bank account.

For women especially, they should look into
alternative treatments or diet and lifestyle changes,
instead of the following surgical procedures:

1. Heart surgery is very dangerous for women.
   It is better to treat their heart conditions with
   medication and appropriate nutrition. Surgery
   produces scar tissue formation, which can
   reduce the effectiveness of this surgery. At the
   very least, take note of this: Women do not do
   well with this type of surgery. Not everyone
   knows why, but women have a very high rate
   of death from this surgery, or any heart surgery.
   Men fare better.
2. Stomach surgery for digestive problems like
   ulcers and the like, may put a person at
   increased risk for getting stomach cancer. This
   was a finding at the Loyola University Medical
   Center. Patients with ulcer conditions that were
   treated with medicines did not have as high
   an incidence of stomach cancer as those who
   had undergone surgery for that problem.
   Avoid liposuction.
3. D & C, Dilation and Curettage-In this
   operation, the neck of the womb is widened,
   and the lining of the womb is scraped off with
   a curette. It is usually done to remove any
   material left after a miscarriage, or to remove a
   tumor or cysts. It can also be used to detect
   possible endometrial cancer, but for this a less-
   expensive test would be a PAP test or an

endometrial biopsy. Again, beware of unnecessary tests. Always ask about the necessity, risks or benefit of any test.

4. Breast Cancer-There are numerous ways that a breast cancer condition may be treated: Radiation, lumpectomy, diet, vitamin therapy including C, E, zinc, chemotherapy, surgical removal. Surgery is just one way, and there is no guarantee that the cancer will not recur. Other treatments are radiation alone, radiation followed by chemotherapy, interferon, hydrazine sulfate, and hormone manipulation. One has to be careful with drugs, as some drugs have caused other cancers, including leukemia.

5. Hysterectomy-This is surgical removal of the uterus. It is said that this operation should not be done unless it is necessary, as serious potential problems could arise in the future. The problems could be physical or emotional. In 2003, a study* found that 75 percent of the 600,000 hysterectomies performed each year were "inappropriately recommended."

6. Gall Bladder Removal-This surgical operation removes gallstones and the gall bladder. However, through a correction in diet, stones may be able to be dissolved and the person may be able to avoid a recurrence of the condition.

Surgery itself involves life-threatening risks.

There can be problems with local or total anesthesia. Whether it's administered as a spinal or an epidural, the placement must be exact. One can be under-medicated or over-medicated with disastrous results. One should always decide if the benefits outweigh all the risks. Communicate with your doctor, get a second or a third opinion if you wish, and educate yourself about it before agreeing to anything. Once it's done, it cannot be undone.

As regards any treatment or surgery that a doctor recommends to you, you should politely, but assertively, ask him questions such as:

1. Do I really need this operation? Why?
2. How soon do I need it?
3. Will it improve my condition?
4. How long afterwards will my condition remain changed?
5. How long will I be in the hospital?
6. What will it cost?
7. What are the risks for this operation?
8. How often do they occur?
9. Are there any other alternative treatments available that can accomplish the same thing?

It is always a good idea to get a second, independent opinion before submitting to an operation, or making up your own mind about it. You do not have to tell the first doctor that you are going to another physician for a second or third opinion, as his or her ego will likely be highly bruised. Remember that you, the patient, would be taking a risk. It's not the doctor who is risking his life, because there is no such thing as 'minor surgery!' Every surgery involves risk.

7

Selected Hospital Problems

One of the greatest threats to a patient in a hospital
is the possibility of getting a hospital-acquired
infection from bacteria or germs of diseases that
other patients have. In fact, hospital infections are
the fourth leading cause of death in the United States
after heart disease, cancer, and stroke. The
Poughkeepsie Journal (July 21, 2002) reported that
hospital infections killed 103,000 people in the year
2000. The Chicago Tribune stated that these deaths
were largely preventable, and caused by dirty,
unclean facilities, germs on medical instruments,
and unwashed hands. Some recent cases mentioned
were a Chicago pediatric medical center where eight
children died, and a West Palm Beach, Florida
hospital in which thirteen cardiac patients died.

A New York Times headline of a few years ago,
stated: "Wash Up!" "Reminder is Often Unheeded."
It seems that many hospital workers are too casual

or careless about washing their hands regularly when going from one patient to another. New strains of common microbes have developed in hospitals, and they are resistant to antibiotics. For example, there is Staphylococcus Aureus. It can be found on the hands of hospital staff workers. A transplant patient, John Allen, was recovering and spoke to his wife about leaving the hospital—except for one thing. He had acquired an antibiotic-resistant staphylococcus infection, which he was trying to fight off. He was dead the next day of septic shock from the massive infection in his bloodstream. It is a strain of Staphylococcus Aureus, which has arisen in hospitals and is now resistant to Methicillin, the best antibiotic for it.

A study conducted at Duke University Medical Center, and printed in The Lancet reported that only seventeen percent of doctors treating people in an intensive care unit washed their hands properly.

In the Annals of Internal Medicine, they reported that the staff rates of appropriate hand washing in a hospital were lowest among those staffers who worked in the high-risk intensive care unit! It is said that this problem is getting worse. Dr. Robert A. Weinstein, director of infectious diseases for the Cook County Bureau of Health Services in Chicago, said, "Hands are the most dangerous thing in the hospital."

New interns at hospitals are usually over-worked, having to tend to many patients and learn quickly how to administer a whole battery of tests that they may never have seen before. For example, on her second day as an intern, a new doctor in New York was quoted as saying; "Yesterday I learned how to set a ventilator for the first time. If I set it wrong, the patient dies. I asked a lot of questions."

A stay at a hospital is often a very frightening, miserable, prison-like experience. You are told to follow their regulations, and strangers take care of you after you've had your clothes removed. Instead of compassion, many patients receive unfeeling and demeaning treatment. There are many indignities to be suffered through, so a patient should seek to leave the hospital as soon as practical. People heal better when they are in their own familiar surroundings at home.

If you have a signed organ-donation form, you should be careful not to sleep too soundly in a hospital. As the comedian Bob Hope once said in this regard, "If you do, you might become spare parts for someone else."

Upon entering a hospital, it's a good idea to bring your Health Care Proxy signed with the required witnesses and give it in to be with your records. Your Proxy Holder is anyone you can trust to carry out YOUR wishes regarding your treatment, drugs and procedures, in case you are incapacitated. Your spouse, guardian, brother, sister, or a friend can be your Proxy Holder to make sure your wishes are made known to the staff, and carried out. For example, you might write on it that you do not want any sedatives, tranquillizers, sleeping pills or painkillers. If you want to make sure you do not get daily blood tests, write that down, and also write that you do not want more than one blood test, x-ray, or whatever else you don't want within a week. Always remember, you have the right to refuse any test or procedure. It's good to speak up. And if you can't speak up, it's even better when it's in writing on a Health Care Proxy. Make a few copies. Give one to the hospital, one to the doctor, and other copies to your nurses and the head nurse.

You should also be careful about signing any papers indicating that you don't want any extra special treatment to keep you alive or save your life. Your DNR order, if you have signed one, can be abused or actually used by doctors to give you substandard care and ultimately to cover up any medical errors they might make regarding your treatment. They would then allow you to die from their errors.

How safe are the IV fluid bags in hospitals? Years ago, Abbott Laboratories were indicted regarding contaminated intravenous fluid bags—where a faulty capping system on several kinds of fluid bags allowed bacterial micro-organisms to live in the fluid even after sterilization took place. Blood poisoning occurred in hospital patients with that intravenous solution. There were fifty deaths and numerous incidences of blood poisoning.

How accurate are lab reports from which your life may be at stake? Many new laboratories have proliferated across the country, and some of the technicians have barely received an elementary school education in this country. Most of the laboratories do accurate work. Sometimes they do not, and people can live or die by the results. For example, when a PAP smear and biopsy of a young girl had a positive reaction, part of her uterus was surgically removed. It was then determined that she did not have cancer. If nothing else, this is an advertisement for more accurate results, and perhaps also for the fact that a young girl, twenty years of age, is generally not an appropriate candidate to get a PAP Test.

In California, a lab tested the blood of a thirty-two year old woman who was in a hospital for surgery. Her blood was reported to be A (Positive). Some time afterwards, another technician re-tested the blood and found that it was actually type O (Positive). However, this second accurate conclusion came too late because the woman had already received two pints of A (Positive) blood during surgery. She died twelve hours later due to an adverse reaction to the transfusions from the wrong type of blood.

A man in Florida had complained to his doctor about continuous, excessive thirst, weight loss, and a lack of energy. However, when the results from a lab came back reporting "No excessive sugar," the doctor said that the man did not have diabetes. Yet, two weeks later, the man went into a diabetic coma and nearly died, except for quick emergency treatment that saved him.

The question of doctor-administered tests is the most important one in this book, because every day doctors give tests on a routine basis which are not only not necessary but which may be harmful. Repeated eye-pressure tests and repeated gonioscopy tests are inherently dangerous. A person's eye pressure changes during the day and night, being lower at night and higher during the day. Some chemicals, or prolonged use of certain ophthalmic antibiotics (for the eyes) may also result in glaucoma. An example is Neomycin Sulfate Dexamethasone Sodium Phosphate.

Some time ago a woman physician was charged with draining millions of dollars from union health plans through big bills submitted for unnecessary tests, as well as for treatment never given. It was charged in a lawsuit against her that she "performed treatments with no medical need . . . including batteries of tests" such as "sonograms and . . . mammograms which were not given." One person was charged $5000 for a vaginal exam. Instead of just a bill for an office visit, there would be a listing of $1200 for tests. To check on her, three healthy men were sent for examinations. She told one of the men he had cancer and needed tests. All were given big bills. One union stopped payment on a $700,000.00 check to this doctor after being concerned that her bills were highly inflated.

8

Practice On The Dying

As if an elderly patient, or any patient, doesn't have enough to worry about (the possibility of deadly infections, the unnecessary tests or x-rays, the excessive blood tests which undermine your immune system and should be declined when in excess), now a report comes out in the open revealing one more horrific hazard to beware of in a hospital. It is this: Doctors practice on dying patients, particularly in emergency rooms when they feel that the person is very elderly and does not, in their opinion, have a long time to live.

What do they do? Unnecessary & invasive procedures, harmful manipulation of the body and excessive blood tests. Someone I know was given more than seven blood tests by a flood of doctors, interns doing their own research at Mount Sinai Hospital in Miami Beach, Florida. It included a test that involves a blood test procedure of threading a tube into the femoral vein in the groin. This sneaky practice test is done without the informed consent of the patient. It is done so that new doctors get to achieve this skill. An elderly patient would, in all probability, decline to be a guinea pig for new interns, so permission is not requested. This particular test is learned best on a person who is alive, so it is done on the elderly person without any concern for his or her welfare, dignity or rights as a patient. The person I know protested, to no avail, because of the pain, and was then labeled as "uncooperative."

Are you safe in a hospital even after you are dead? No, because other procedures, techniques and tests may be tried by interns and residents on newly deceased patients. They have been seen practicing the insertion of breathing tubes into the throats of patients who have just died. This is also, of course, done without the informed consent of the (dead) patient. Families are not usually told about any of these medical training procedures done on their loved one, whether that person is dead or alive.

It is dangerous to be a patient in a 'teaching hospital' because new doctors and interns are learning on you! Many of them are from foreign lands, and there may be miscommunication between patients and foreign medical personnel.

The potentially harmful practice sessions on hospital patients who are coming in to get well or to recover, just serve to promote, inculcate, and sustain malevolent, dishonest and unethical attitudes in doctors just beginning their professional life.

9

Medical Experimentation

Every day, researchers, doctors, hospitals and universities do research studies with live human volunteers. The same possibilities of medical errors, incompetence or incorrect judgments and mistakes that abound in the medical arts, put these research subjects at risk of becoming seriously ill or dead. The death of Ellen Roche in an asthma study shows these risks quite clearly. She was part of an experiment conducted at Johns Hopkins University School of Medicine, At their asthma and allergy center, she had to inhale an experimental drug compound, as instructed by the principal research investigator, Dr. Alkis Togias, Associate Professor of clinical immunology. Ms. Roche was a healthy twenty-four year old technician who worked at the university. The first subject who inhaled the drug, Hexamethonium, became ill, then recovered, but Dr. Togias did not report this to the Board that was overseeing the study. Ellen Roche, the third subject to inhale it, died. After spending several weeks in an intensive care unit, during which time her lungs stiffened and leaked air, and her organs started to fail, her family ended her life supports.

Omitted on the consent forms signed by the volunteer subjects was any information that the drug could damage a person's lungs, that the drug's safety was in doubt, and that the drug was not approved by the FDA—the Food and Drug Administration. The consent form merely said that the drug's main risk was a temporary decline in blood pressure, and it omitted the real life-threatening results. A report on this was sent to the government's Office of Human Research Protection.

Another volunteer subject, involved in a gene therapy study at the University of Pennsylvania, died as a result of that research.

There have also been other deaths and disastrous results in other research areas such as diet studies and skin research. A healthy woman who was a volunteer for an Alzheimer study died after being given a common dietary supplement (possibly an excessive dose) in this research project. It was at Case Western Reserve University in Cleveland in 2001.

10

Euthanasia

This nice-sounding word actually represents something which is not so nice: the practice of aid to the dying—to help them die faster. Some states have had this on the ballot, to allow doctors to speed up the dying process in patients whom they think have a few months to live, and who have requested help in this regard.

Plainly speaking, euthanasia is "a doctor's license to kill." As journalist Charles Krauthammer wrote in an article some years ago, "the killing will not stop with the extreme case of the terminal patient. It only starts with him." He states, "A license to kill inevitably corrupts the doctor and endangers the patient."

Permitting euthanasia in hospitals or in doctors' offices would let out a Pandora's Box of evils. Firstly, it would easily be a cover-up for any and all doctor or hospital-caused errors on any healthy patient or any patient who is not terminally ill. If the patient dies, the doctor could write in the records that the person was terminally ill with a heretofore undiagnosed condition or that the person had given the doctor oral permission (or written permission if the doctor forges the patient's signature on a "permission to kill" paper).

The Netherlands is one Western nation where euthanasia is tolerated, although still illegal. From reports by the Dutch government's Committee to Investigate the Medical Practice of Euthanasia, during a particular year, they listed 2300 cases of voluntary euthanasia and over 1000 cases where the doctors deliberately hastened death 'though the patient has submitted no explicit request for that.' It appears from the Dutch government's investigation that there were several factors that propelled the decision of the doctors to end a patient's life without the 'explicit request of the patient.' Two of the factors listed were, "Low quality of life"—31%, and "The family could no longer take it."

There were cases where doctors decided that certain people were better off dead, that their lives were not worthwhile—despite the fact that these people had not put in any requests to be killed by their doctor. They may have considered children with Down's Syndrome or Parkinson's patients not fit to live; or, people with Alzheimer's disease as immediate candidates for euthanasia.

Once you let this euthanasia out of the box and give doctors a license to kill, it cannot be contained or controlled. It can only proliferate into a corrupt, deadly practice of forged papers and medical abuse cover-ups. Investigations would only be after-the-fact, and people would be dead by then. And if it was a patient's verbal request to die, a dead patient could not corroborate the truth of that request. It might be done for economic reasons, or the doctor might deem an Alzheimer patient to have an unworthy quality of life.

11

Life Or Death Blackboard

In point of fact, there are probably many hospitals in the United States that already practice a form of euthanasia. They do this by withholding or withdrawing treatment for a patient whom they consider to be terminally ill, and allowing that person to die. Obviously in most cases this is against a person's wishes because patients go to a hospital and incur big expenses to recover from illnesses, not to languish without care, and die.

A few years ago it was revealed that the Memorial Sloan-Kettering Center had a secret 'Life or Death Blackboard'—an erasable chalkboard—on which they wrote the names of patients whom they were going to allow to live or die! The news, which came out about their secret, was that they were considering abandoning this practice. Yes, after the secret was in the public domain the hospital's deputy physician-in-charge, Dr. Thomas Fahey, said, "The Medical

Board of the hospital is going to address this, to codify exactly what our policy would be in these situations."

On the 'Life or Death Blackboard', patients whom they were going to allow to live were marked A and B. Those marked C and D were to be allowed to die. This latter classification was presumably in place apart from any written DNR (Do Not Resuscitate Order) which the patient himself or herself may have given to the hospital.

The secret 'Life or Death Blackboard' was located inside the doctors' private lounges.

Do you want a doctor to decide whether you should live or die? Do you think they should play God and assign themselves the right to terminate a life? It is clear that when you go to a hospital, you have to worry: "Will I be cured or killed?"

12

Legalized Suicide

Oregon has this country's first physician-assisted suicide law, called the Death with Dignity Act. Any Oregon resident who has been diagnosed with an illness that would indicate he or she has less than six months to live, can get a doctor's prescription for an oral, lethal drug. The person, within a time frame of fifteen days, must make one request in writing and two oral requests. A second physician must confirm the terminal illness, and the patient must be considered to be mentally capable.

It is hard to argue against a terminally ill person's right to suicide, but there are many ways for potential wrongs when it is backed up by law. For example, a poor family may want to hurry a relative's death for economic reasons. Retarded or handicapped people might be pressured into the direction of physician-assisted suicide. Health insurance companies might financially promote physician-assisted suicide and withdraw coverage for certain types of care or treatment, thus narrowing a severely ill person's ways to recover, and pushing him or her closer to suicide.

13

Malpractice, Mishaps & Murder

This section of the book includes a variety of medical errors, malpractice, mishaps, murder, maltreatment, negligence, abandonment of care, callousness, physician arrogance, substandard care, medical bungling and incompetence which caused grief to many families and resulted in patients' suffering and/or death.

As usual, an investigation into patients' complaints against doctors often takes years to complete. In the meantime, the inept, incompetent doctors keep practicing their profession, causing the deaths of other patients.

Case 1

One such case was that of a thirty-four year old woman who went to the Southampton, Long Island offices of Dr. Michael Morrissey for a breast implant operation. An hour and a half after she was given

an overdose of anesthesia, she was taken to a hospital.
Nine days later she was dead—dying, according to
investigative officials, from Dr. Morrissey's
negligence.

Case 2

The same Dr. Morrissey above, one year later,
was preparing a twenty-one year old woman for a
similar operation in his Yonkers, New York practice.
Not long after administering anesthesia, the woman's
blood pressure dropped and her pulse could barely
be heard. This emergency started at 8:20 A.M., but
the woman was not taken to Physicians Hospital in
Queens until 3:30 in the afternoon. She died without
regaining consciousness. This doctor's license was
revoked a full year after the Southampton case. Had
his license been revoked sooner, the second woman
would not have died in the same type of operation.

Case 3

In Syracuse, New York, at Crouse Irving
Memorial Hospital, a fatal drug error took the life
of a judge's wife. The sixty-four year old woman,
Muriel Simons, was supposed to be given Paraplatin.
Instead, a more powerful drug, Platinol, was given
to her—and given in overdose. This caused her
kidneys to fail, she lost her sight and hearing, and
died. Investigators could not determine if the error
was caused by the pharmacist who prepared the
drug, or by the nurse who injected it. The two drugs,
Paraplatin and Platinol have been added to the

journal called Hospital Pharmacy's List of Look-alike or Sound-alike Drugs.

No one in the hospital who was involved in this case was fired or reassigned, and the state decided not to fine or discipline the hospital.

Case 4

A different result occurred in Ohio where indictments of involuntary manslaughter and reckless homicide were brought against two defendants after the deaths of four nursing home residents, who were given nitrogen instead of oxygen, ostensibly by mistake. The tragedy took place at the Carriage by the Lake Nursing Home in Bellbrook. The four died of nitrogen asphyxiation.

There were six other residents there who became sick after a nitrogen tank, mistakenly delivered to the nursing home, was attached to their oxygen system. The nitrogen's tank label actually had an oxygen label on it, which was partly covered by a small *Nitrogen* label.

Case 5

In Connecticut, at the Hospital of Saint Raphael in New Haven, two women died as a result of being given nitrous oxide, by mistake, instead of oxygen. The patients had been in the hospital for cardiac catheterizations. How did this happen? The meter that controlled oxygen was wrongly plugged into a container of nitrous oxide, also known as laughing gas. The resultant tragic deaths were not funny.

Case 6

In another case, an anesthesiologist revealed to both state and federal investigators that he worked in hospital operating rooms for many years while being 'stoned.' The state Health Department was chagrined that federal investigators had not relayed this information to them, as they believed this doctor, Dr. Neil Ratner, was a public health threat.

Case 7

In Stony Brook, Long Island, a baby just six days old died as a result of being given ten times the amount of potassium chloride. It was supposed to be 3.5 mg. Instead, 35 mg was administered. One can wonder if the individual who made the mistake got his position through affirmative action.

Case 8

A similar incident occurred at the National Institutes of Health Clinical Center to a 20 month-old boy. He died one day after he was given a saline solution that contained five times too much salt. A correct amount of salt in the solution had been prescribed, but two nurses and a supply room worker misread the order.

The solution was meant to treat an ear infection the boy had developed. The mistake started when a clerk misread the prescription and took out "the wrong bottle" which had a 5% saline solution instead of a normal 0.9% saline solution with 5% dextrose. The next error occurred when a nurse hung up the wrong bottle at 10 P.M., without realizing it was wrong. A third error was made at 4 A.M. by the night nurse, who put another bottle of the excessive saline solution in place. The boy went into a coma, and died exactly one day later at 10 P.M. His parents said they were going to sue for 35 million dollars.

Case 9

An eye doctor in Queens, New York, partly blinded a patient of his as he pretended to remove non-existent cataracts from this person. His ostensible motivation for the operation was money, which would be paid by Medicare. Dr. Shaul Debbi was charged with trying to defraud Medicare after he did the same surgery on ten patients. For example, one patient who told the doctor he had vision problems, had 'cataracts' removed from both eyes. The doctor also caused the man's eyesight to be damaged afterwards as a result of his assorted operations.

Case 10

The legendary, resourceful artist, Andy Warhol, met his death in New York Hospital-Cornell Medical Center on February 22, 1987. Fifty-three year old Andy had gone to this hospital to have a gall bladder operation on February 20th and had the surgery the next day. He hired a private nurse to be with him during his hospital stay, as an extra precaution—to be sure he would be safe and that all his needs would be taken care of. However, the hospital failed to continue monitoring Andy Warhol during the night following his operation; and the nurse he had hired to watch him, fell asleep. It was sometime after midnight when he had problems as a result of the operation, and died. His private nurse was in the room, but had fallen asleep.

Case 11

In the same hospital where Andy Warhol died, George Ball went in for tests, and died. His family was going to investigate why he checked in but did not check out. Carlton Fredericks, the former nutritionist, once said, "A hospital is a place where you go in vertical, and you come out horizontal." Many years ago the 'giant' Eddie Carmel went in for hospital tests. He died at Montefiore Hospital at the age of 36. This type of thing—dying from tests—is not an uncommon occurrence. It's just underreported as such.

Case 12

Tonsillectomy operations used to be very common in the 1950's and 60's, but today's conclusions are that they should be limited to children who have actual problems related to the size of their tonsils, or various throat infections.

A few years ago, a four-year-old girl had a tonsillectomy as an outpatient procedure, and went home. The next day, she had fever, and died four days later after coughing up blood. She had bled to death. The child had seen an H.I.P. pediatrician after her fever began. Then she went to a different hospital where she died.

Bleeding is the major complication of a tonsillectomy and it happens either within 24 hours after the surgery or seven to ten days later when the scabs are falling off. The child should have been properly monitored.

Case 13

Next is the case of a woman whose death was reportedly laughed about, as her family has charged, in the emergency room at New York's Mt. Sinai Hospital, where during part of one year over 123 complaints of patient care were received by the State Health Department. Selma Messinger was a retired teacher who had two previous surgeries at that hospital—one for a tumor in her neck, and a second operation to take out infected tissue at the area. Now she was going back because of two fainting spells three days afterwards.

At the Mt. Sinai Emergency Room, the staff neglected her. Within six hours, she collapsed. Despite two doctors finding her to be dehydrated, records show she was not given any fluids until she was in the emergency room for five hours.

Her cardiologist from the medical team, Dr. Edward Fisher, was called, and he told her to call Dr. Mark Urken, her surgeon. In addition, according to Mrs. Messinger's son Andrew, Dr. Fisher told the family's private nurse not to call him again "unless she's in cardiac arrest." The surgeon did not answer the family's telephone message that night. Another surgeon at the hospital told them to come to the emergency room the next day, which they did, arriving after noon. Mrs. Messinger told the emergency room staff she was thirsty, but they refused to allow her to have any water. They said, "We have to check with the doctor." When Dr. Fisher arrived at 2:30 P.M. he found Mrs. Messinger to be dehydrated, and said that she should be given fluids and be examined by an Infectious Disease Specialist, and he left. She was placed on a cot, and, despite the instructions, was not given anything to drink. The family pleaded with the staff, but was rebuffed, with the staff again saying they had to check further. After five hours, the infectious disease specialist saw her and okayed her discharge. But when her oxygen was removed and she was preparing to leave, she fainted and was taken to a bed as she recovered. A curtain was extended and security guards had the family go outside the room. Records show that this was the first time that she was given fluids. They were given intravenously. At about 5:45 P.M., the family saw members of the staff rushing behind the curtain. Then the emergency room chief came out and said, "She's dead." The surgeon had come a few minutes before, and Dr. Fisher was there. A fight broke out, and the Messinger family members were shoved to the ground and beaten by the hospital security guards, as reported by the family. Police were called. Family members, only one at a time, were then allowed to see their dead mother. A glass of water, given when she requested it, may have saved her life.

Case 14

A more famous case in a hospital emergency room took place some years ago at New York Hospital. A young girl named Libby Zion, age eighteen, arrived at the hospital's emergency room. She had a fever of 103.5 degrees and was allegedly "writhing and agitated."

In that emergency room, she received substandard care, in that she was not given appropriate tests to determine if an infection was present. Then, a hospital resident, after deliberating with an emergency room resident, had her admitted to the hospital. The doctors were told that she had been taking Nardil, a strong anti-depressant.

For all of the treatment that followed Libby Zion's hospital admission, her care continued to be done by a young inexperienced doctor and nurse who were in training.

She was placed in bed and tied with restraints to suppress her writhing. Her temperature at some point rose to 107 degrees, but no doctor checked on her regarding this. She was given an injection of Demerol. The combination of Demerol and Nardil is a deadly one—but one which none of the resident trainees bothered to realize.

Libby suffered greatly because of the inhumane treatment, the fatal mistakes, and the "woefully" inadequate care as presented in a report by a Manhattan grand jury. The New York Post called the hospital arrogant.

Within eight hours at the hospital, Libby Zion was dead of cardiac arrest.

Case 15

The importance of making sure that doctors do not transfer germs or diseases from one patient to another can be seen clearly in this case. A former anesthesiologist, Dr. Marvin Chiumento, of Bay Ridge Endoscopy and Digestive Health Center in Brooklyn, apparently administered anesthesia to a patient who had chronic hepatitis C. Afterwards, he reused those same hypodermic needles and vials over and over again on other patients. As a result, an investigation revealed he had thus given nineteen other people hepatitis C.

Case 16

A Florida woman went to a surgeon for a face-lift. She apparently suffered brain damage, went into a coma, and then died. Another woman said that this surgeon, Dr. Alton Ingram, punctured her intestine and nicked her pancreas while she underwent a liposuction procedure. She had to go to a hospital to rectify the condition. Still another person said this same doctor disfigured her.

The doctor had no malpractice insurance, and he filed for bankruptcy.

Case 17

This next case cries out for less carelessness and more education for doctors. A man went to New York's Mt. Sinai Hospital for a heart operation, and died. The ensuing investigation is going to determine whether his death resulted from the doctor allegedly installing the aortic valve upside down, the delayed surgery to place it correctly, or other reasons.

A heart surgeon exclaimed that putting in this particular prosthetic device could be confusing after it is removed from its holder (the package) in which its proper position is seen.

The chief surgeon in this case had recently been attracted from Harvard Medical School to supposedly earn a seven-figure annual paycheck at Mt. Sinai. This situation can show, when the investigation is completed, that neither a doctor's age, experience, nor paycheck has much to do with a patient's life or death.

Case 18

In Tampa, Florida, at University Community Hospital, a woman was partially sterilized without her consent. It was done after a Caesarean section birth and was stopped by a nurse who noticed it being done and reminded the doctor that the woman had not given her consent to sterilization. It wasn't until the media confronted the hospital that the hospital admitted the "error."

This hospital has also been told to tend to "immediate and serious" threats to patient welfare as seen from the death of one man who was wrongly removed from a ventilator, and the amputation of the wrong foot of another man thereby assuring the man's remaining years on earth as a double-amputee, a paraplegic!

The man on the ventilator had been mistaken for another patient. The president of the hospital, in "An Open Letter to the People of Tampa Bay," wrote in part; *"Unfortunately, in health care, mistakes happen . . ."*

Case 19

In Miami, a man went in for 'minor surgery'— to remove a benign tumor near his thyroid. In the recovery room, he choked on his own blood more than twenty minutes before it was noticed. Then a nurse called the surgeon. An anesthesiologist used an unsuitable drug to clear his airway, and the surgeon came too late. The patient wound up in a coma. He is now paralyzed and unable to speak, all because of mistakes from 'minor surgery.'

His family sued, and a Dade County jury awarded him six million dollars.

Case 20

When wondering what else can happen in doctor-patient situations, how does this sound: A doctor falling asleep during operations. A doctor from Long Island, who was alleged to have fallen asleep during several operations, gave up his New York State physicians' license rather than face a variety of charges.

His hospital privileges at Parkway Hospital were suspended after he had fallen asleep while administering anesthesia to patients. A conversation he had with another doctor who saw him fall asleep was the deciding factor in this case, in which there were other problems as well.

Case 21

A respiratory therapist is supposed to help patients breathe. This therapist, however, tried to make sure some patients under his care, at Glendale Adventist Medical Center, did not breathe.

The former respiratory therapist in southern California, Efren Saldivar, injected patients with a drug used to paralyze them—before attaching them to respiration equipment. He tried to achieve patient deaths without clues.

Mr. Saldivar avoided execution by pleading guilty to six fatal poisonings (first degree murder), and one attempted murder. Previously, he had confessed to 50 "mercy" killings of elderly patients, and then retracted his statement of 50 and reduced it to six deaths.

He was sentenced to life in prison, with no chance of parole.

Case 22

A woman in Brooklyn was improperly cleared for gallbladder surgery. The admitting physician at Beth Israel Medical Center noted she had an enlarged liver and advised further tests to be done. However, the surgeon did not adequately review the patient's records and she was set up to have surgery the following day.

After the surgery, she began to hallucinate and thereafter had liver and kidney failure. It was said that hospital doctors then decided to have Dr. A. S. Greenberg alter the woman's chart in the eventuality of a lawsuit. In other words, to lie.

At the trial, the defendants said that the woman would have died in any case. They claimed that the surgery and general anesthesia she was under did not worsen her liver condition.

A six million dollar verdict was announced to the dead woman's husband and children.

Case 23

Whoever said that tests—especially those incorrectly done—have no consequences? An eight months old boy went to a hospital in Queens to be tested for spinal meningitis. For this test, a needle is inserted into the spinal cord and some fluid is extracted. This test went awry because the nurse bent the child's head too far forward and his oxygen supply was cut off for at least three minutes.

The boy suffered cardiac arrest and went into a coma for eleven days. As a result of the brain damage, the boy was left blind, mentally retarded, and paralyzed for the rest of his life. He is now a quadriplegic and is fed by way of a tube.

His family won a judgment of 27.5 million dollars.

Case 24

In Watertown, New York, a hospital was sued by a woman who charged that it lost part of her head. A portion of her skull had been temporarily taken out so that doctors could tend to an aneurism inside her head. The piece was six inches by two inches and was reportedly lost. This, claimed her lawyer, would subject her to possible future health hazards and medical expenditures.

Case 25

Peggy Cass, an actress, went in for an operation on her left knee. This sounds simple, but it wasn't simple for her doctor at Lenox Hill Hospital in New York. He operated on her right knee (the good knee) instead of her left knee.

When Ms. Cass awoke in the recovery room after the operation, she saw bandages on her right knee and none on her left knee. She realized the mistake. She was returned into surgery for another operation, this time on her left knee, which was what she came in for.

A jury awarded her $460,000 for having suffered through this preventable mistake.

Case 26

Several years ago, the mother of pretty movie star, Sridevi, of India, was in a hospital for the removal of a brain tumor. Rajeswari Ayyappan had traveled half way around the world to come to America for this medical procedure.

What happened in this tragedy in New York, at the Memorial Sloan-Kettering Cancer Center, was that the neurosurgeon cut into the wrong side of the patient's brain by mistake. The reason given was that he took the wrong patient's x-rays into the operating room, which caused him to open the wrong side of the head.

As a result of this tragic medical error, the hospital will be undertaking several reforms in an attempt to prevent a repeat of this horror. The surgeon and the head nurse will now have to sign a checklist indicating that they have the correct medical records and correct x-rays for that particular patient. They must then take that data into the operating room.

The patient went to New York Hospital afterwards where the correct side of her skull was opened and the tumor removed.

Case 27

Do you think operating on the wrong side of the head is a rarity? Think again. Since 1995 over 150 doctors have made this type of mistake. There have also been cases of operating on and removing the wrong leg, cutting off the wrong breast (the healthy breast) and even operating on the wrong eye.

A doctor in Providence, RI, also operated on the wrong side of the head. This occurred after a CAT-scan was set out backwards on an x-ray viewing machine.

Case 28

What about a doctor operating on the wrong eye? A woman went to Flushing Hospital in New

York for a procedure to help restore her sight with a corneal transplant on her left eye. After the operation, she woke up and discovered to her horror, that her good right eye was the one covered with bandages. That is when she realized that her healthy eye had been operated on and was now badly damaged. As a result, she has two bad eyes instead of one. The doctor offered to do the operation again—on the correct eye. The woman refused, and said she would sue.

Case 29

You always have to be sure you're getting the operation you are in for—if you must have it done, because there are chart mix-ups, similar-named people, etc. At Rhode Island Hospital, a girl was supposed to have eye surgery. Instead, the surgeon removed her healthy tonsils and adenoids, by mistake.

In Miami, Florida, a woman who had the same last name as another woman, had the wrong chart, did not get her insulin and other appropriate medications, and died as a result.

Case 30

If I had to choose the saddest malpractice case I have ever heard of, it is this one. It is about a girl named Misty Lowenthal. When she was twenty-eight years old she had gall bladder surgery. As she said, "It was supposed to be a simple operation, but after four days, when anybody else would have gone home, I was still in the hospital screaming and yelling in pain." The doctors persuaded Mindy's parents that she was "crying wolf." They exclaimed, "Oh, she's just being Sarah Bernhardt."

However, Misty wasn't acting. The reason she was in such terrible pain was because an infection had developed as well as a number of other complications, so doctors had to operate on her again. After this second surgery, they told her "gangrene had set in" and her "stomach had exploded." They also told her she would "never be able to eat again," because her stomach, small intestine and most of her colon had to be taken out in that operation. Her esophagus was closed so no food could go down. Mindy explained, "I have to feed myself intravenously." She had repeated infections, and was propelled into that miserable, disabled condition for life. She became deeply in debt from all the procedures and visits to the hospital and had to sue them for medical expenditures, pain and suffering. To a newspaper reporter who interviewed her in 1987, she said, "The slaughter in our streets by handguns is not as great as the slaughter in our hospitals at the hands of negligent doctors." She told him, "I try to make jokes and be happy . . . but it's hard."

Doctors told her that some day she would have to receive kidney dialysis. Misty Lowenthal's pain and agony ended four years after the messed-up gallbladder operation. She thereby saved the hospital a lot of money by dying, as they no longer had to be concerned about reimbursing her for any further medical expenses, lost earnings or pain and suffering. Her suffering ended September 15, 1991.

Case 31

When a person's life is at stake, one would think that doctors and hospital staff would be careful and accurate in administering powerful drugs. From the 'best' hospital to the 'worst,' medical errors and malpractice go on unabated.

Betsy Lehman was a patient who was in a hospital to receive a bone marrow transplant to kill breast cancer cells. She was at the prestigious Dana Farber Cancer Institute in Boston, and her husband worked as a scientist there.

Unfortunately, thirty-nine year old Betsy Lehman, the mother of two small daughters, was given a fatal dose of an anti-cancer drug. She received four times the correct dosage, four days in a row. Warning signs, lab tests, and electrocardiogram results were missed. The horrendous error went unnoticed by all doctors, nurses, and pharmacists. Betsy Lehman, who had great hope of success in this hospital, died quickly from the overdose.

Case 32

I will say this: No surgery is really minor, no medical procedure is minor, and no doctor's treatment is minor.

Years ago, Rick Sklar, who was a WABC-AM radio consultant in the 1960's, went to a hospital for an elective 'minor' foot operation. It was for a torn tendon on his left foot.

Medical bungling ended Rick's life quickly. What happened? A tube was placed incorrectly, and it pumped air into his stomach in place of his lungs!

His anesthesiologist, Dr. L. Helmer, did not notice it and neither did a broken patient-monitoring machine—for twenty minutes. Rick Sklar became unconscious on the operating table, had an inflated stomach, began choking, suffered cardiac arrest, went into a coma and died. He had gone to the hospital June 21st and died June 22, 1992.

What is even worse about this case is the revelation that the hospital attempted a 'cover-up' by withholding some of the details and even recording a "false entry" from the monitoring machine that was broken at the time of Mr. Sklar's operation! Outrageous!

Case 33

As noted in the previous case, there is nothing 'minor' or 'routine' when it involves medical procedures.

The famous sportscaster and author of more than 30 books, Dick Schapp, went to Lenox Hill Hospital in New York for replacement hip surgery.

Something went wrong with the operation and a serious complication occurred: acute respiratory distress syndrome. His lungs failed; ultimately he became unable to speak. He was placed in the intensive care unit where he lay for thirteen weeks, and died on December 21, 2001.

His son Jeremy said, "It's unbelievable. He was perfectly healthy when he walked in, other than a sore hip . . ."

Case 34

Nowhere can the callous, dangerous, indifferent treatment of a patient be seen more clearly than in the case of Dr. James Watt. A young woman, Leah Grove, went to see this doctor for treatment of a mild case of depression. She went to improve her life, not to die. Dr. Watt used his experimental "carbon dioxide therapy" on Leah. She went into cardiac arrest in the doctor's office. He tried to resuscitate her, while her friend called 911 for help. The friend had accompanied her to the doctor's office.

Leah died. Dr. Watt's medical license was surrendered, and he pleaded guilty—to criminally negligent homicide. This appears as a classic example of a rogue character hiding behind the title of 'Doctor.'

Case 35

A case of physician indifference and callousness was that of Dr. David Benjamin toward his patient, Guadalupe Negron. She had heavy internal bleeding after an abortion procedure. A paramedic was with her afterwards but did not speed to the hospital, once the doctor had told him there were no complications—just "minor bleeding." It appeared the CPR may have been done ineptly, which forced fluids into her lungs, and a breathing tube put in the wrong way. The doctor was also accused of causing gashes to her inside organs such as the uterus and her cervix, etc. because he miscalculated the size of the fetus. He probably avoided telling the paramedic the truth about the serious gashes and dire hemorrhaging in order to cover his mistakes.

He was put on trial for murder.

Case 36

In this case of incompetent medical treatment, a young woman, Roxanne Murray, went into a hospital to give birth. She began to bleed badly in the recovery room at Kings County Hospital Center, after the birth by Caesarian section. She apparently did not receive adequate care. Eventually she went into a coma and died. Her family was awarded 3.9 million dollars.

Case 37

Beverly Stevens' family was awarded 41 million dollars "to be paid by New York City." She died several hours after an Emergency Medical Service ambulance crew refused to carry her down her stairs.

Ms. Stevens was on a visit to New York from her home in Kingston, Jamaica. She started to experience stomach pain and went to Kings County Hospital. She told them she was several months pregnant. After two visits there, she was diagnosed as merely having a urinary tract infection.

Days after her last hospital visit, she was at her sister's apartment and suddenly buckled over in pain.

A telephone call to 911 brought an ambulance. The EMS ambulance crew refused to carry her down. Another ambulance crew came out but Ms. Stevens was dead by then, having died within an hour and ten minutes.

It was later discovered that she had an ectopic (outside the womb) pregnancy, which the hospital had failed to diagnose.

The 41 million dollars award was one of the highest jury payments in New York State.

THE NEXT FEW CASES nearly all deal with pregnancy, Caesarian births and birth defects from malpractice, mishaps, and substandard medical care. Due to fear of malpractice suits, obstetricians are performing more baby deliveries by Caesarian section. They feel there is a smaller chance for complications through cutting open a woman's stomach for childbirth. What they don't want you, the patient, to know is that a Caesarian section is major surgery, with a chance of many complications that can accompany any surgery. In addition, there is higher mortality for women who agree to this unnatural way of giving birth, especially in older women. Also, babies taken out too soon can have cerebral palsy, weak muscles or breathing or mental retardation; However, there are some legitimate times for C-section deliveries—but not for the fear-of-lawsuit reasons that motivate many doctors.

A government report by the Centers for Disease

Control and Prevention in Atlanta has said that the number of childbearing deaths in America has been greatly underestimated—that it is likely twice as high as that reported.

On a final note, a doctor may not force you to have a Caesarian section (C-section), even to supposedly save an endangered fetus, if you—the patient==do not want to bear a child in that manner. Many doctors also overstate the danger to a fetus in an effort to persuade a pregnant woman to agree to do things his way. The Illinois Supreme Court refused to allow a woman to be forced to have a C-section. Her religious beliefs were involved in her decision not to undergo a C-section even though the doctors said her fetus was not getting enough oxygen (in their opinion) and might have brain damage before being born.

Doctors have ways to try to force women into having C-sections, sometimes with lack of truthfulness, other times by other methods. I know of several cases like that. In one, a woman was in labor a long time and was not interested in the surgery risk of a C-section. The doctor then told the head nurse and other hospital staff members not to tend to that woman and to deprive her of anything she might want, even if it's a glass of water. He then went to try to get a Court Order from a judge. When he returned to the hospital, the baby was being born naturally.

A study in The Lancet medical journal found a risk of stillbirth for the second baby in women who had their first babies by Caesarian section.

Case 38

Some of the complications of pregnancy and childbirth leading to maternal deaths are: hemorrhage, blood clots, pregnancy-induced high blood pressure, infection and cardiomyopathy, a type of heart failure. Kathy Kerr, the wife of a Philadelphia Flyers hockey player, Tim Kerr, died at age 30, a mere ten days after she gave birth to a child by Caesarian section. She developed an infection for which the hospital claimed she received treatment, but then had a "sudden cardio-pulmonary complication" according to a University of Pennsylvania Hospital spokeswoman.

Other speculation about the exact cause of her death centers on the possibility of a traveling blood clot, perhaps from her infection site to her lungs. It is said that death after childbirth is often from an embolism. It can be caused from the surgical procedure of C-section itself, or from excessive blood tests at the hospital. These types of tests possibly hold more dangers after childbirth and surgery, than before.

Case 39

A woman took her infant son to a hospital for treatment due to an asthma attack. She thought she would be there for a few hours. Yet, because of a medical mistake at Broward General Medical Center, she was unable to take the child home until he was twelve years old!

The medical mistake had left him paralyzed, blind, and unable to speak. When she finally took her son home, he was like a little shriveled doll, and was as small as a five-year-old boy. His mother, on his behalf, received a six million dollar settlement from the state Legislature. What good is the money if you are blind, paralyzed and cannot speak because of medical errors?

Case 40

A doctor's misdiagnosis left one triplet brain-damaged. What happened to Beth Myers is that a condition of hydrocephalus—fluid on the brain—occurred after the birth. There were complications, which developed after the doctor's procedure to allow the fluid to drain into the abdomen. She was rushed to an H.I.P. Medical Group where a doctor said she was suffering from a milk allergy.

It turned out that Beth Myers had the abdominal infection called peritonitis. As a result, she suffers from cerebral palsy, has to use a wheelchair, and is legally blind.

A jury awarded her 56 million dollars because of the misdiagnosis.

Case 41

A pregnant New Jersey woman was told that she had an abnormal PAP smear. After repeated PAP tests, one after another, it appeared that a cancer had developed. She was advised by her doctor to end this pregnancy a few weeks before her due date, so that the cancerous cervix, the uterus, and ovaries could then be taken out at the same time.

The doctor was sued on the basis of being too aggressive in wanting the early delivery, and that he did not get an appropriate informed consent from the woman. The jury award at the trial was for 43 million dollars.

Actually, the mental retardation of a child, as in this case, is a classic result from a birth that is induced too soon. Other results can be cerebral palsy, muscle weakness, and problems with speech.

Case 42

Having inadequate or substandard care from either experienced or inexperienced doctors is bad enough, but when you are a voluntary living donor in a hospital, you are facing a substantial risk to your life. People still do it.

One such case, of liver transplantation, involved two sisters, Joann DeMichiel and her sister, Pauline, who donated a portion of her liver to the younger sister, Joann.

The operation took place at New York's Mt. Sinai Hospital, where there have been numerous deaths in transplant cases, and the hospital has been fined sixty-six thousand dollars recently by the state, and cited for numerous violations and deficiencies.

Joann De Michiel died almost a year after her operation. The day before she died, she was quoted as saying, "I wouldn't hesitate, if I had to do this again, to go there."

Case 43

One patient, Anthony Montemarano, who went to the hospital for a liver transplant died before receiving any such operation there. His family said the liver ward was "filthy." They revealed that the staff did not take out a tube, which was drawing blood in his arm when he told them it was bothering him. Then afterwards he had an infection. Doctors were at a loss to explain the reason for this man's death at Mt. Sinai Hospital. Many other families have voiced the same concerns about Mt. Sinai Hospital. Lack of cleanliness, inexperienced doctors, ignoring patient requests and inadequate care were some of the many problems they discussed.

Case 44

Another recent transplant situation, at Mt. Sinai Hospital in New York, also had an unfortunate ending. It was also a liver transplant case between siblings, two brothers. This time, however, it was the living donor, the older brother Mike Hurewitz, who died—only three days after the surgery. He was a very healthy man, a marathon runner. The younger brother who received the liver section is recuperating.

Mt. Sinai Hospital is one of the leading liver transplant institutions, but there have been many deaths in their transplant cases, in both the recipients and the living donors. The New York State Health Department's investigations of these tragic cases at Mt. Sinai have revealed "serious quality of care issues" for recipients and donors. On the day of the

Hurewitz death it was learned that a new doctor-in-training was left with the care of thirty-four patients. Complications can occur afterwards, such as infection, blood clots, bile duct injury, and the most serious, liver failure.

The Health Department said that Mike Hurewitz received "woefully inadequate" post-operative care. It was said that his vital signs were not recorded properly. Also, when a doctor was paged and heard that Mike Hurewitz' condition was deteriorating, he dallied in a bookstore as if trying to stay away from a sinking ship. But this was no ship. This was a patient—a liver transplant donor. These operations reportedly cost $300,000.00 each. When the doctor came back to the hospital, he did not go to Mike, but went instead to another patient who was to have surgery the following day!

Mt. Sinai Hospital afterwards instituted changes in its liver donation program such as: No care is to be given to transplant patients by interns or first year residents; doctors will have to respond to pages within five minutes; the ratio of nurses to patient will go up to one to four, and other changes.

Mt. Sinai Hospital was fined $48,000 as a result of his death and nearly 100 other complaints of abominable medical care. Sixty-seven other deaths are being investigated. On August 30, 2002, the hospital was fined $66,000 for thirty-three deficiencies found by the New York State Health Department. In addition, they ordered liver transplant surgery to be suspended indefinitely. It is unclear if it has been resumed, but the saying "fools rush in where angels fear to tread" might apply here.

It's too late for Mike Hurewitz, but others will be saved and doctors might learn to be more caring of lives.

Case 45

A recent case regarding the hospital death of 12-year-old Michael Tyler Fisher in New York, demonstrates the gravity of going to a hospital whether you are young or old. (It's worse if you are older, as hospital personnel may think you've lived long enough).

Michael went to Westchester Medical Center in Valhalla, New York, last January because he had a bad headache. It was about nine o'clock in the evening. Due to medical errors regarding powerful drugs he was given, he never returned home. He died, apparently from "acute mixed drug intoxication."

Michael had been given Morphine—a respiratory-suppressant and dangerous life-threatening drug, and Fentanyl (Duragesic) which is another powerful pain killer, not really recommended for children. His parents claim he was not monitored afterwards.

The boy is dead, and the hospital—which denies any wrongdoing—is being sued for 100 million dollars.

Case 46

Here is a very interesting case. It began with a thin, ninety-three year old man who had a stroke which caused right-sided arm/leg muscle weakness. He was taken to the Emergency Room at Sound Shore Medical Center of Westchester in New Rochelle, New York, where CAT scan pictures indicated a stroke. He was not given TPA, but was given blood tests and later on the dangerous drug, Heparin, a blood thinner. The next day, for no compelling reason, he was taken to an MRI tank for pictures of cerebral areas already sufficiently covered the day before. This test appeared to be extraneous, and if it was, then it was an abuse of the patient and Medicare. With no regard for the possible, probable, and highly likely harmful consequences of a sedative drug overdose, this patient's doctor, Stanley Holstein, ordered not one but two sedative/tranquillizing drugs in quick succession: a total of 15 mg. of Valium and 4 mg. of Ativan. Dr. Holstein wanted the patient, an elderly man, to be 'perfectly still' for the MRI test.

Afterwards, heart, lung and all muscle functions were suppressed by the combination of the two drugs, each drug dose being an overdose by itself. Together they represented a powerful synergistic mechanism. The sedation thus effected by that overdosage of drugs was such that the patient lost consciousness and went into a coma for three days. The patient was never given an antidote. His Health Care Proxy Holders were never given prior notice of the sedation, and thus never gave their permission for the drugging. The patient awoke late on the afternoon of the third day after a family member kept a radio playing loudly for six hours. Upon regaining consciousness, the patient was unable to stay alert, or speak; swallowing was compromised, eye function was distorted, and all muscular structures were further weakened and 'tranquillized' by the heavy sedation. He got hospital-acquired pneumonia the next day. Weakened by the sedation ordered by Dr. Stanley Holstein, as well as by a blood supply drained by endless daily blood tests, he went into a downward spiral. Any stroke patient, whether in this hospital or elsewhere, who gets overdosed with sedatives and tranquillizers and excessive daily blood tests will be a very weakened person with a depressed immune, circulatory, respiratory, cardiac and muscular system. And those conditions can only represent a stumbling block to a stroke patient who is intent on recovering muscle function and strength for standing and walking. Instead of assisting recovery, Dr. Holstein impeded the recovery of a patient entrusted to his care. The overdosages ordered were akin to attempted murder. Stroke patients would likely do better at home with hydration, aspirin therapy, speech, physical and occupational therapy.

Case 47
Another case, similar in some regards to the previous one, was that of an older woman who

voluntarily checked into Mt. Sinai Hospital in Miami Beach, Florida, for 'heparin treatments' that her doctor could "monitor." It was followed by similar disastrous results. Beginning on the first night, a Cuban nurse gave the patient her medications on an empty stomach, despite the patient's protest. "Kitchen closed" was the nurse's reply. What followed after that was vomiting, cardiac/respiratory stoppage, then a recovery that lasted until the patient got hospital-acquired pneumonia, then went home after recovery. But the damage had already been done to the patient's stomach and body. Weeks later the patient returned on a Sunday night to Mt. Sinai Hospital Emergency Room, to get Zantac, a drug which was then only available by prescription. After a minimum of seven blood tests, one after another at this 'teaching hospital'—where interns perfect their testing skills by practicing on many elderly patients, she expired.

Case 48

Here we have a set of proven, willful, deliberate murders of patients by a doctor. An inquiry found that over a 23-year period he killed 215 of his patients. The sweet, sympathetic, kind-looking man is Dr. Harold Shipman, a general practitioner for many years. There is no need to worry about this dangerous doctor, because he has been convicted of crimes, is currently serving fifteen life sentences, and will never be eligible for parole.

No clear motive for his crimes was ever given, but

he told one woman patient's family after killing her, "I don't believe in keeping them going." The investigators found that of the 494 deaths of Dr. Shipman's patients, he killed a minimum of 215 of them. They said, "The true number is far greater and cannot be counted." There were at least 45 other suspicious deaths of the patients of this trusted family doctor.

Dr. Shipman began killing his patients one year after beginning his medical practice. He became addicted to murdering his patients, and did it from 1975 to 1998. The ages of his victims ranged from 41 to 93 years; 171 were women, and 44 were men. Suspicions of this doctor came to light when he forged the will of his last patient, Kathleen Grundy, whom he killed.

This trusted doctor often went on "house calls" to his patients who were usually at home alone. The patient may have called him, or he may have decided to visit for a routine examination. He would then use one of his methods of killing, which was usually an injection of fatal doses of heroin or the painkiller Diamorphine, and the like. The patient might be left sitting on a chair, or on a sofa at home. He sometimes reported the death to the family. He would then return to the scene, totally nonchalant, and had a ready answer for each sudden death.

The prosecutors at his trial explained that his behavior was necessitated by the need for "godlike power over life and death."

The inquiry into Dr. Harold Shipman also stated, "Other well-marked traits of Shipman's personality were aggression, conceit, arrogance and contempt for those whom he considered to be his intellectual inferiors." The entire report can be seen online at *www.the-shipman-inquiry.org.uk*

The people in Hyde, England were consoled in their anguish by the tolling of the church bells 215 times, but how many more Dr. Harold Shipman's are lurking around unfettered?

14

Patients' Bill of Rights

1. Right to considerate and respectful care in a clean and safe environment free of unnecessary restraints.
2. Right to know the name and position of the doctor in charge of your care.
3. Right to know the names, positions and functions of any other staff involved in your care, and refuse their treatment, examination or observation.
4. Right to receive complete information about your diagnosis, treatment, and prognosis.
5. Right to receive all the information you need to give Informed Consent for any proposed procedure or treatment, including the possible risks and benefits of the procedure or treatment.

6. Right to Refuse Treatment and be told what affect this may have on your health.
7. Right to a no smoking room.
8. Right to refuse to participate in research and experimentation.
9. Right to privacy in the hospital, and confidentiality of your information and records.
10. Right to participate in all decisions about your treatment and discharge from the hospital. The hospital must provide you with a written discharge plan and written description of how you can appeal your discharge.
11. Right to review your medical records and obtain copies for a fee.
12. Right to receive all the information you need to give informed consent for an order not to resuscitate. You also have the right to designate an individual to give this consent for you if you are too ill to do so.
13. Right to know the hospital regulations.
14. Right to receive treatment without discrimination.

Medical consumers must never forget that they have "Patients' Rights." These rights have been backed up by law, and have at times had to be enforced in the courts. Know your rights, and even carry this with you to medical facilities for your own protection always. Specific patients' rights may vary in each state. Find out what the rights are for a patient in your particular state.

Health Care Proxy

(1) I, _____

hereby appoint _____

_____

(name, home address and telephone number)

as my health care agent to make any and all health care decisions for me, except to the extent that I state otherwise. This proxy shall take effect when and if I become unable to make my own health care decisions.

(2) Optional instructions: I direct my agent to make my health care decisions in accord with my wishes and limitations as stated below, or as he or she otherwise knows. (Attach additional pages if necessary.)

_____

_____

_____

(Unless your agent knows your wishes about artificial nutrition and hydration (feeding tubes), your agent will not be allowed to make decisions about artificial nutrition and hydration. See instructions for samples of language you could use.)

(3) Name of substitute or fill-in agent if the person I appoint is unable, unwilling or unavailable to act as my health care agent.

_____

_____

(name, home address and telephone number)

(4) Unless I revoke it, this proxy shall remain in effect indefinitely, or until the date or conditions stated below. This proxy shall expire (specific date or conditions, if desired):

_____

(5) Signature _____

     Address _____

     Date _____

     Statement by Witnesses (must be 18 or older)

     I declare that the person who signed this document is personally known to me and appears to be of sound mind and acting of his or her own free will. He or she signed (or asked another to sign for him or her) this document in my presence.

     Witness 1 _____

     Address _____

     Witness 2 _____

     Address _____

15

Conclusion

During the course of their careers, many doctors have developed arrogant attitudes toward patients, and feel they are above criticism. They play God so many times that they begin to think they are superior to lay people and that they know everything; but they do not.

At the very least, many doctors are lacking in person-to-person skills. They often talk down to patients, and are angry or annoyed when patients offer their opinions. They pretend to listen, but they do not. More importantly, they withhold information, and do not communicate adequately with patients.

Doctors make more money by limiting the amount of time spent with each patient. With less time, the quality of care suffers, patients become abandoned, and careless, preventable errors occur. That is when medical care can kill you.

Anyone who believes in staying away from

doctors is in good company. Albert Einstein had only one serious invasive medical procedure, and did not trust doctors. Thomas Edison refused to have any operation or treatment for his deafness; and the centenarian Delaney sisters of Mount Vernon, New York, also avoided doctors nearly all of their long lives, both living in good health over one hundred years.

When very old, healthy people were asked what they attributed their longevity to, most of the answers included:

1. Eating a good breakfast every day.
2. Awaking at the same time every morning.
3. Going to bed at the same time every night.
4. Getting enough sleep.
5. Exercising several times a week, or walking briskly every day or every other day.
6. Eating lots of fruits and vegetables.
7. Maintaining a low-fat, low-cholesterol, low-calorie diet.
8. Following a low-salt, low-sugar diet. Eating yogurt, and garlic.
9. Being optimistic.
10. Staying away from doctors.

Helpful Hints to Avoid Doctors:

Angioplasty and Bypass Surgery for Women

Balloon-Angioplasty is a procedure which is very risky, and has high death rates for women. Men fare better. Therefore women should try nutritional changes in their diet: oat bran, wheat germ, bioflavonoids, fibrous fruits, celery, cauliflower, brussel sprouts and other cruciferous vegetables, and low-dose aspirin therapy twice a day. Also they should avoid sugary foods, hard, hydrogenated or trans fats, and high cholesterol foods such as butter, margarine, lard, coconut oil, palm kernal oil, egg yolks, regular ice cream, regular milk, potato chips, butter cream, whipped cream, and hard cheeses. Eat much less.

Cancer

The National Cancer Institute advises on ways to stay healthy and prevent the disabling diseases of cancer, stroke and heart disease. They urge people to avoid too much sugar, salt, alcohol, hydrogenated oils or fried foods, trans fats, saturated fats and cholesterol; to eat a variety of foods, and keep an ideal weight. Fats promote cancer, so it is best to avoid being obese. Daily exercise such as walking is recommended. A diet high in fiber, and low in fat will decrease the risk of cancer, as will whole grain breads, cereals, oat bran, celery, fruits, dark green and yellow vegetables. Cigarette smoking increases the risk of cancer.

Researchers in Canada have reported that low-dose aspirin (81 mg.) taken once a day, or less often, may lower the incidence of colon and rectal cancer. Eating a diet with sufficient bran and fiber-rich foods is also helpful.

Gallstones

For prevention and/or the possible dissolution of gall-stones, one should drink plenty of fluids, cut out fats and cakes, lose some weight, exercise more, have more fiber in your diet, and take large doses of vitamin C. Lemon juice with water also helps.

Glaucoma

Stress, family history, and high intraocular (eye) pressure (IOP), are possible precursors to the onset of glaucoma. High IOP alone may not trigger glaucoma, whereas other factors will bring it on quickly. Any eye injury, sometimes cataract surgery, certain medical conditions, and direct pressure on the eyeballs, including the pressure put upon the eyeballs by eye doctors' tests, can cause glaucoma. Whether the doctor is pressing a gonio lens on the naked eyeball, or the puff of air test, or the Goldmann tonometer pressure test, there are consequences for the eyes which are not beneficial. You may leave the eye doctor's office with anything from bloodshot eyes to the possibility of glaucoma within 24 hours. Eye tests may also increase eye pressure.

Besides cutting down stress through yoga, meditation, or relaxation with music, eyes can benefit from good nutrition, especially the B, C, and E vitamins, oranges, kale, tomato sauce, corn, red and orange peppers, kiwi fruit, blueberries, bilberries, carrots, squash or sweet potatoes, peaches, apricots, strawberries and spinach. These carotenoids also help prevent macular degeneration, as well as improving eyesight. Omit salt. Space fluid intake. Exercise! Avoid dark movie theaters.

Heart Attack

Lots of things contribute to a heart attack. They include emotional stress, anger, temper outbursts, sudden heavy physical activity, inactivity or lack of regular, moderate exercise, above-average body weight—especially in the waist/stomach, high cholesterol meals leading to clogged arteries (arteriosclerosis), diabetes, high blood pressure and smoking.

Ways to improve your odds of avoiding or surviving a heart attack are to lose weight, exercise on a regular basis such as walking, etc., cook with liquid vegetable oils such as canola oil, have meals of fish, skinless poultry, breads, cereals, oat bran, skim milk, fruits, walnuts, apricots, bananas, apples, raisins, pears, and eggs (no yolks). Avoid salt, creams, fats, and potato chips. Have fish at least once or twice a week, and cruciferous vegetables from the cabbage family. Have several portions each week of brussel sprouts, cabbage, broccoli, cauliflower, rutabagas, turnips, kale, asparagus, red peppers, mushrooms, sweet potatoes, green beans, carrots, celery, onions and tomato sauce. Have citrus fruits and juices to be sure to have enough vitamin C (especially lemons and oranges), and take a vitamin and mineral pill and garlic—perhaps daily. Avoid mayonnaise, pickles, sausages, ham, bacon, pork, duck, veal, shellfish, lamb, spare ribs, frankfurters, luncheon meats such as liver, liverwurst, salami, bologna, corned beef, tongue, smoked salmon, smoked meats, olives, sauerkraut, soy sauce, hard cheeses, processed cheeses, croissants, butter rolls, salted snacks, butter, lard, coconut or palm oil, and hydrogenated fats. Daily low-dose aspirins may prevent heart attacks. Use a larger uncoated dose immediately upon getting a heart attack to reduce any damage. Lastly, get a pet, real or stuffed.

On the cholesterol issue, there are two types of cholesterol. LDL is the 'bad' cholesterol and should be less than 130 mg/dL, or under 100. HDL is the 'good' cholesterol and should be over 45 mg/dL. These are just general approximations. Your total cholesterol level should be below 190 or below 200 mg/dL. Add olive oil to some foods to reduce cholesterol.

Hemorrhoids

These are swollen veins in the anus, the lower part of the colon. It may be hereditary or a result of dietary, lifestyle, and toilet habits. Excessive straining during bowel movements, or infections, or sitting for too long a time can cause it. Sometimes it occurs after a pregnancy. Do not scratch the area. Instead, use a cotton swab or a clean finger to lubricate the area with petroleum jelly or vitamin E oil you've squeezed out of an opened vitamin E pill. If there's bleeding, you can apply a bit of witch hazel with a cotton ball. A 10-15 minute warm bath will help. Wear cotton underwear. Losing weight will reduce the pressure. As to diet, decrease salt intake, increase fiber and drink plenty of fluids. Vitamin C (by mouth) can help keep the stools soft. Take 15 to 30 g. per day, or use a stool softening medicine. Using hemorrhoid cream is considered better than a suppository. It is said that a diet rich in unprocessed bran can prevent hemorrhoids (piles). Fiber-rich foods include whole-grain breads and cereals, beans, celery, fruits—including dried fruits, and vegetables.

High Blood Pressure

You can lower your blood pressure by losing excess weight, doing aerobic exercise daily (walking, biking, swimming), and eliminating smoking. Meditation and relaxation techniques can be done to soothe stressful times. Eat onions. They contain a substance that can lower blood pressure. Have garlic or garlic supplements. Calcium, magnesium and potassium-rich foods are also beneficial. Milk, bananas, and apples can act as natural 'tranquillizers.' Reduce salt and sugar in your diet. Actually, try to avoid salt. Studies have shown blood pressure going up even higher with sugar than with salt. Canned soups and frozen meals have astronomical amounts of salt. Look at the labels. Do not use any table salt on your food. Avoid anything with caffeine. It is found in coffee, tea, cocoa, chocolate, soft drinks, as well as in some prescription drugs. Noises have also been shown to cause blood pressure to rise significantly and to remain high for even weeks after the disturbing noises. Stay calm and happy, talk less (talking raises blood pressure), and relax to reduce hypertension (high blood pressure).

Osteoporosis

As you get older it's important to do exercises such as brisk walking, jogging, and stair climbing for bone-building. Otherwise you will lose calcium in your bones. Foods rich in calcium include vitamin D fortified milk, raw spinach, kale, tofu, almonds, sardines, canned salmon with bones, nuts, citrus fruit juices fortified with calcium, and broccoli. People over 65 years of age need at least 800, more likely 1500 International Units of calcium per day. An 8 oz. glass of milk has 125 i.u. Four ounces of canned salmon have about 565 i.u. of calcium. One should stop smoking and limit the intake of caffeine, alcohol, meat, phosphates (in sodas, etc.), and salt. Those who do not go outdoors often to get vitamin D from the sunshine, or those who do not exercise enough, are at risk of calcium deficiency.

Pregnancy

Medical/surgical mortality rates are higher for those women who have Caesarean sections rather than normal childbirth. It can be up to 26% higher in some places. Here are other possible outcomes. If you have a Caesarean section for your first child, and you have a second child in the future by VBAC, there's a higher chance it could be stillborn. Or, you could go into premature labor, followed by an emergency Caesarean. You could get endometritis, a serious infection of the uterine lining which could result in infertility or a hysterectomy operation. You may need a blood transfusion. Most women who die from C-sections lose their lives from too much loss of blood or infections resulting from this life-threatening surgery. Always ask a doctor, "What is your rate of Caesareans?" Tell him/her if you do not want it. Also ask, "How do you deal with dystocia (stalled labor)?" Does the doctor seem glad to answer your questions, or is he unwilling or in a hurry?

You do not want to be a death statistic from this major surgery, so be assertive in your statements to doctors in order to avoid an unnecessary Caesarean section. Learn to say "No."

Prostate Health

There have been several "home remedies" to keep prostate cancer at bay. One is to lose weight. Other research indicates that tomatoes or preferably, tomato sauce prevents and fights prostate cancer. Other preventives include pumpkin seeds, sunflower seeds, hard boiled eggs (no yolks), mushrooms, and low dose of zinc supplements. Some recommend an aspirin (low-dose) a day.

Different treatments are available for prostate cancer, depending on the stage the disease is in when it is first discovered. One is brachytherapy when it's early, another is 'seed' implantation, and still another is Avastin which cuts the tumor's blood supply. The latest advice is to drink green or black tea.

Sleep Improvement

Here are several ideas for greater success in falling asleep. Going to bed and getting up at the same time every day can help you sleep better. It is important to get up at the same time each morning. Use fresh bed sheets and sleep in a neat, darkened room. Exercise regularly but not before your bedtime. The bedroom temperature should be about 65 degrees Fahrenheit, if that is comfortable for you. Avoid smoking or drinking alcohol before bedtime. Do not have any coffee, tea, cola, soda, or prescription drugs for several hours before your bedtime. It's better to drink a glass of warm milk with half of a banana or a muffin. The amino acid L-tryptophane in milk induces sleep.

A warm bath, and a few minutes of reading is a good aid to sleeping better. If any of this does not work, get up for awhile before returning to bed.

You can also sit down and do yoga exercises,

meditation, deep breathing, counting to 100 then counting backwards, or hypnotizing yourself, and relaxing before bedtime.

Stroke

The current hospital treatment for clot-type strokes is IV injected heparin which they 'monitor.' By 'monitor' is meant repeated blood tests on the patient every six hours (sometimes in addition to other blood tests), day after day—lowering the patient's immune system and red blood cell supply in the process. This is a possible ticket to death, especially when it's done in a hospital, the hotbed of all of nature's vilest germs, bacteria, and diseases.

To save your life, and take care of the above type of stroke, stay home and keep hydrated by drinking water and fruit juices and take aspirin every day. Check with your health care professional as to dosage, whether it should be coated aspirins or not, and how many per day. Find out about the new blood-thinning drug, Exanta. Have your affected muscles massaged daily, get physical/occupational therapy, and speech therapy for any swallowing (myofunctional) or speaking problems. Your chances for survival will likely be far greater at home than in a hospital with their current mode of treatment.

Travelers are advised to walk around and stretch during a long trip, to improve circulation and avoid blood clots leading to a stroke. Take a coated aspirin before a confining trip.

Varicose Veins

For mild cases a few things can be beneficial: sit down and use a footstool for your feet; use a pillow under your feet to elevate them occasionally when sleeping; do leg exercises to improve circulation, and take walks. Believe it or not, most doctors do not recommend surgery, because after they remove some varicose veins, other veins may become varicose. In that case you are back at square one, and have undergone surgery, which is not a plus, since scar tissue can be a problem afterwards. Support stockings worn during the day can help.

Final Note: Unneccessary or unwarranted tests, examinations, and operations are very risky. "Routine" medical treatment by doctors can kill you or ruin your life. A visit to a doctor is an appointment with danger.

Selected Readings

Christensen, Bryce. The Family in America—article, Vol. 18, Number 2. Rockford, Illinois: The Howard Center for Family, Religion and Society, Feb. 2004*

Fleming, Michael F., M.D. and Archer, Victor E., M.D. "Ionizing Radiation: Health Hazards of Medical Uses." Consultant—The Journal of Medical Consultation. Vol. 24, No. 1, p. 167-184, Greenwich, CT: Cliggot Publishing Company, 1984.**

Gott, Peter, M.D. No House Calls. New York, NY: Pocket Books, 1986

Healing With Nature. Emmaus, PA: Prevention Magazine, 1980

Hearth, Amy Hill. The Delaney Sisters' Book of Everyday Wisdom. New York, NY: Kodansha America, Inc., 1994

Horowitz, Lawrence C., M.D. Taking Charge of Your Medical Fate. New York, NY: Ballantine Books, 1988

Mann, Eric. Hazards of Medications.

Marks, Edith & Montauredes, Rita. Coping With Glaucoma. Garden City Park, NY: Avery Publishing Group, 1977

Mendelsohn, Robert S., M.D. Confessions of a Medical Heretic. New York, NY: McGraw Hill Company, Re-published 1990.

Norwood, Christopher. How to Avoid a Caesarean Section. New York, NY: Simon & Schuster, 1984

Physicians Desk Reference

Rosenblatt, Stanley M. Malpractice and Other Malfeasances. Secaucus, NJ: Lyle Stuart, Inc., 1977

INDEX

Abdomen, 27, 31, 35, 56

AIDS, 11, 37

Alzheimer, 70, 72-73

Angiography, 27

Angioplasty, 123

Asthma, 42, 48, 69

Ataxia, 45

Blood clots, 42-44, 131

Blood pressure, 41-43, 45, 50, 52, 70, 80, 127-128

Blood test loss, 16, 46-47, 67, 110-111, 131

Bone marrow, 33

Bradycardia, 30

Breasts, 33-34, 57, 79

Cancer, 27, 34, 43-44, 57, 61, 65, 97, 123

Cataracts, 27, 45, 83

CAT scans, 33, 36, 94, 109

Cerebrovascular insufficiency, 30

Cervical biopsies, 27

Chest, 33, 35

Cholesterol, 50, 126

Dental, 34-35

Depression, 45, 52

Diabetes, 30, 39, 43, 65

Diarrhea, 45

Dysarthria, 45

Eyes, 27-32, 41, 44, 66, 80, 83, 92-95, 110

Gall bladder, 56, 83, 91, 95

Gall-stones, 124

Glaucoma, 27-28, 30-31, 42, 48, 66, 124-125

Heart, 28, 30, 41, 43-45, 50, 56, 61, 125-126
Hemorrhage, 27, 85
Hemorrhoids, 126-127
Hepatitis, 37, 88
HIV, 16
Hypotension, 30
Hypotonia, 45
Hysterectomies, 57

Irritability, 45

Jaundice, 45

Kidneys, 28, 30, 35, 42, 44-45, 48, 92

Liposuction, 56
Liver, 35, 41-43, 45, 48, 92, 105, 106-108
Lumps, 27
Lungs, 45-46, 50, 70, 90-91

Mammogram, 33, 34
Memory loss, 45
Meningitis, 92

MRI, 33, 44, 109
Muscular weakness, 45-46
Myopia, 45

Nearsightedness, 29

Orthopedics, 27
Osteoporosis, 128

Pneumonia, 49
Pregnancy, 27, 56, 89, 99, 100-105, 128
Prostate, 129-130
Ptosis, 31, 41

Reproductive organs, 33

Sleep improvement, 130
Spine, 35
Spleen, 45
Stroke, 16, 49, 55, 61, 110, 131

Thyroid, 33, 36, 90
Tonsillectomy, 84
Transurethral biopsies, 27
Tumors, 27, 90, 93

Varicose veins, 131

Vascular collapse, 45

X-rays, 32-36

Drugs

Adalat, 51
Alcaine, 28
Alcohol, 41
Alteplase, 49
Ambien, 47
Antibiotics, 42, 66
Aspirin, 44, 50, 110, 124, 126, 129, 131
Ativan, 47-48, 109
Avastin, 130

Barium enema, 35

Calan, 51
Cardizem, 51
Cortico-Steroids, 30, 42
Cosopt in a solution of Mercury, 29
Coumadin, 49

Dalmane, 47
Demerol, 87
Dexacaine, 28
Diamorphine, 112
Dilacor, 51
Diltiazem, 50
Duragesic, 108

Ephedrine, 52
Exanta, 49, 131

Fentanyl, 108
Fluorescent dye, 28

Heparin, 49, 109
Hexamethonium, 69
Isoptin, 51

Librium, 47
Lorazepam, 47

Morphine, 48, 52, 108

Nardil, 87
Nifedipine, 50

Paraplatin, 80
Pilocarpine, 29
Platinol, 80
Procardia, 51

Restoril, 47

Selfotel, 48
Streptokinase, 49

Tetracycline, 42, 48
TPA, 49, 109
Tranxene, 47

Valium, 47, 109
Verapamil, 50
Verelan, 51

Xanax, 47
Zantac. 111